# The Runes:

# A Grounding in Northern Magic

# THE RUNES

**The Runes**

A Grounding in Northern Magic

Written and illustrated by James Flowerdew

ISBN 9780993227271

First published in 2021 by The Magic Road,
an imprint of Leamington Books

The moral rights of the author have been asserted.

Production Manager: Joshua Andrew
Editorial: Ambrose Kelly

Leamington Books
32 Leamington Terrace
Edinburgh

Typeset in Garamond / Elder Futhark J

Printed and bound by Imprint Academic, Devon

# Contents

# Illustrations

# Introduction

This book is an introduction to the Runes and has been written for many reasons. Many good books on this subject already exist - yet there commonly seems to be a gulf between academic Rune books and practical Rune books.

Many of the more practically orientated Rune books are just too simple and don't back up what they tell you, which means that it's hard to say whether you're reading facts or someone's personal fictions. With a system as mysterious as the Runes, these instances of intuition or guesswork can pose a problem and may set many off on the wrong course.

On the other hand, it's nice to have information explained clearly - a task which many academic rune books seem to struggle with. I have always taken the attitude that if you are unable to explain your ideas to someone else, it is likely that these ideas are not very well understood by yourself.

This book will give you a faithful representation of the Runes with their individual meanings, as well as how they work as a system.

It is difficult to approach any spiritual subject and not have a personal sway. But rest assured, I will endeavour to at least tell you where wild leaps of intuition (or foolishness, maybe?) are made, and where personal opinions are my inspiration.

Where possible, sources of information will be provided so that you can come to your own conclusions concerning any theories offered.

Runic magic and culture is largely thought of as Viking culture. Some call this knowledge 'heathenism', and others prefer the phrase 'the Northern tradition'. The focus of this book  is a little more complex than this – however, we are going to talk about Vikings and Northerners a lot.

Much of this information is grafted from Icelandic literature, a source which many believe to be the most relevant body of surviving text with the least tampering. The most reliable material we have for detail on the Runes is mostly Viking. This material is reliable because it is ample, well maintained and old. The majority of these Viking records are thought to have been authored some time between the 9th and 13th century CE (Common Era).

However, some rarer finds which can date back as far as the 3rd century BCE (Before Common Era) and spread all over Europe at least. Then there is related material that goes back further still. In some cases, this archaeological evidence may be cited although this book is not intended to be an archaeological study of the Runes.

Additionally, this book contains some allusions to popular folklore. Certain Pagan or 'heathen' ideas survived in the minds of ordinary people long after Christianity moved north through Europe. Many traditions were maintained around the fireside in the form of stories and customs, where they were all but obliterated in written text. For many ancient peoples, the spoken word was more sacred than written text, meaning that many ideas probably never made it into written form.

I am no trained historian, but, like all good rune users, I have invested myself in them for many years. In providing as many of these sources, as close to their origin as I can, I hope to achieve the clarity and honesty that I would personally seek in a rune book. While I am not a well seasoned writer, I am confident that 'interesting' won't be a challenge. I can let the Runes do that job themselves. If I can make the Runes boring, that in itself deserves honour of some sort.

# What are the Runes?

The word 'Rune' - likely derived from the Sanskrit word 'run', meaning 'secret' or 'whisper' - is often used to describe any esoteric or indecipherable symbol. However, 'Rune' has been particularly attached to the ancient alphabet associated with historical Viking and Saxon peoples.

These 'Runes' are a collection of symbols used to convey two sets of information. In addition to their phonetic values for use in writing, they represent distinct elements of a universal cosmology in both physical and spiritual ways.

As far as we can tell, they were always treated in this dualistic way, as tools for both every-day writing and magical, or spiritual, use.

Viking legends frequently refer to them being used for magic by mortals and gods alike.

There are many different related versions of this alphabet. The most commonly recognised and used set of characters is called the 'Elder Futhark', which consists of 24 different symbols.

The word 'Futhark' (pronounced "foo-thark") simply means alphabet, and is likewise constructed out of the following first characters thus:

Alpha + Beta = 'Alphabet'
Feoh + Ur + Thorn + Ansur + Rad + Kaon = 'Futhark'

# The History of the Runes

## *An Important Background*

In order to understand the origins of the Runes, one must be familiar with some ancient history. This is important, as some common conceptions of pre-Christian Europe make the ideas behind the Runes seem unusual to the modern mind.

You will have heard of the Bronze Age - an era starting around 6,000 years ago in the regions between Iran and Egypt, spreading out and then collapsing 400 years before the rise of the classical nations.

People of this time are wrongly perceived as a mix of isolated savages and ignorant tyrant kings. This view is not strictly true. In reality, people have been sophisticated in many ways for much longer than you might presume.

Vitally, it is called the 'Bronze Age' because many cultures used bronze. Bronze is not a simple metal, but an amalgam of copper and tin which most of these nations had to import over long distances, (commonly from either Cornwall or Afghanistan). Thus, as long ago as five or six thousand years ago, we can see that many cultures including the Egyptians, the Hittites, and the Indo-Europeans were trading on a scale of thousands of miles.

There are plenty ancient examples of this long-distance trading. We know that the Egyptians had amber, and that in Orkney they had wine.

You cannot grow grapes on Orkney. That means good boats, currency, communications, able carpenters, sailors, and indeed the

RUNES

knowledge that wine and amber exist. All of this on or available even on remote islands in the middle of the North Sea.

Why am I saying this? Primarily, because the ancient Pagan world was not stupid, isolated or ignorant. These communities communicated with each other, sharing technology, medicine and ideologies. There is plenty of evidence of this, even communications in the form of letters and other records survive – often multilingual.

Thus, the ancient world was a more connected environment than we usually imagine, and the Runes are a part of this. The Runes evolved from not only from distant geographical sources, but they were part of a long-running global discourse.

# The Legend Begins

*"Wounded I hung on wind-swept gallows,*
*For nine long nights,*
*Pierced by a spear, pledged to Odin,*
*Offered, myself to myself*
*The wisest know not from whence spring*
*The roots of that ancient rood*
*They gave me no bread,*
*They gave me no mead,*
*I looked down;*
*With a loud cry*
*I took up Runes;*
*From that tree I fell."*

No one truly knows where the Runes came from. To many etymologists, the studiers of texts and written language, all that can be derived so far is this:

- The runic alphabet was created independently and was not directly evolved from another written script.

- The earliest runic texts were found in southern Europe, the knowledge probably taken north by the Germanic tribes.

Some believe the Runes to be inspired by the Etruscan alphabet, which was used by the ancient people of Etruria (modern Tuscany and Umbria, Italy) between the 7th and 3rd centuries BCE.

In some cases, there is also similarity to Latin letters of the same value. This hints at the inventors of the Runes being aware, at least, of Latin, which has so far been dated back to the 6th Century BCE.

Some people relate the Runes to the ancient Indian language, Sanskrit, which is thought to be our closest intact relative to Proto-Indo-European. Proto-Indo-European is the name for the theoretical common ancestor of most modern European and Indian languages, including Latin. This direct connection to Sanskrit is unlikely, as whilst many European words are closely linked to Sanskrit — allegedly including the word 'rune' itself — the runic Futhark has stronger parallels with the Semitic alphabets, such as Aramaic, Phoenician and Hebrew.

As an aside, it is also worth mentioning that the 13th century Icelandic scholar Snorri Sturluson stated a belief that the Norse gods were Trojans. On first hearing this, my instinct was to believe that he was attempting to connect himself to the classical world. Perhaps, I thought, he was struggling to imagine his own environment as a good home for culture. However, later research has highlighted similar writing systems and strangely familiar gods in the vicinity of what is now modern-day Turkey. Jupiter Dolmenicus, as the Romans called him, is a good example — he resembles Thor a little too much for comfort.

However, the Runes were claimed by their ancient users to have been discovered by Odin — king of the gods. The story goes that in a Shamanic style ritual of self-discovery, Odin hung for nine days and nine nights on Yggdrasil, the tree of life, without food or drink, and wounded with a spear. On the ninth day, he saw into the primal abyss and was able to grasp the Runes out from the beginning of time.

Unlike Latin, Greek, and Persian alphabets, the Runes were never seen as solely a text for writing, but as a system for magic and mystical understanding. They were developed with this in mind, which brings us to another interesting theory.

Many runic practitioners argue that the Runes were developed to encourage ancient European shamans and mystics to record their knowledge in a coherent fashion, which they refused to do in other written alphabets.

Thus, they argue, a system was created that could be used both phonetically and symbolically. Many of the Runes are certainly based on symbols that go way back in history to beyond what conventional archaeology claims to understand. These have existed in their own rights, or have similar signs that have been found in ancient art the world over, so the Runes could well be an attempt to bring together all of the forces of the universe as seen by ancient man in one system.

This is backed up both by the fact the Runes have names that reflect meanings, but also by various rune poems, which date back at least 500-1000 years. These poems share a belief in the symbolic nature of the Runes and, while their content does differ, they have enough in common to suggest an earlier more unified system. We will discuss these in greater detail later.

# A European Language

While the oldest available uncontested Runic scripts date back to the 1st century BCE, the Runes seem to be at their most widespread during the 11th Century. Most runic finds date to this period. Archaeological evidence shows the Runes being commonly used throughout Europe, from the Balkans to Germany, Scandinavia, Great Britain and Iceland at this time.

At this stage, a variety of new Runic Futharks emerged as various cultures adapted them to suit their own languages. These various forms of runic writings were used for almanacs, graffiti, scriptures, memorials, spells, charms and decorations — among many other uses.

The simple angular shapes of the Runes made them easy to write and carve on a variety of surfaces such as wood, rock and metal, as well as on parchment and leather.

This meant that the Runes belonged as much to the labouring classes as they did to the leisured classes — those who tended to be the masters of literacy in most ancient cultures. The Runes' magical power therefore seems to have been classless, and not just the privilege of the wealthy elite. Much of the information presently known about the Runes was passed down through the folk culture of ordinary people. People bore runic charms and gave their children Runic names, such as Dagma (the day), Ethel (the home), Rowyn (famous friend), Astrid (divine beauty) and Ingrid (beloved). They also built runic shapes into their buildings, temples and later, churches.

Notably, one of the reasons the Runes and their magic survived at all, was the fact that rural peoples, 'pagans' (peasants) or 'heathens' (heath dwellers), carried on using their ancient practises long after the supposedly more enlightened leisured classes had moved on to Latin Script, and Judaeo-Christian ideologies.

In remote areas of the Balkans, the Runes were still used for almanacs in the early 20th century. In Great Britain, people hammered nails into posts for good luck well into the 19th Century, which was traditionally an invocation of Thor — and blacksmiths were entitled to perform weddings because of the same connection with Thor and his hammer.

Iceland was more able than most European countries to preserve its ancient history, and the legends and traditions of the Viking peoples were able to quietly co-exist with the Christian community. Here, Snorri Sturluson used common folk tales and poems to re-construct some of the best-known records of legends of the Viking gods and kings. Iceland is also the home of the Codex Regis, or Elder Edda, although it was discovered in Denmark.

Today, the official religion of Iceland is now formally Odinism again. Admittedly, this is a recent change, as It was Roman Catholic for most of the Middle ages, and indeed, at the time of Snorri Sturluson. Iceland however is the only place in Europe where building plans can be inhibited formally, on account of fairies allegedly inhabiting the site.

# Dark Days, and the Fall of the Old Ways

With the spread of Christianity, many old religions and cultures were stamped out of existence. As the new faith swept over Europe aided by its new champions, the Byzantine Romans, the face of Europe was changed forever.

This is a common theme in human history, where arriving cultures attempt to oust the faiths and ideologies of the older by displacing their gods — but this was on a new scale. Pagan cultures tended to demote gods and religions, but early Christians obliterated all the knowledge of their predecessors in order to substantiate their ideas as predominant.

The Runes were seen as a threat to the reformed and newly Christian Roman Empire, led initially by the Frankish King and Emperor, Charlemagne. This new Roman Empire saw the Teutonic Runic systems as non-Roman, and thus savage.

The Empire also wished to promote the idea of Latin being a holy script for the divine aristocracy - peasant runic literacy was seen as a threat, and thus, evil.

Strangely, perhaps in an effort to assimilate it and remove its Pagan content, Charlemagne even commissioned a separate Christian set of Runes, now called the 'Later Gothic' Futhark. This possibly indicates that the Runes were more widespread than Latin in many areas of Europe in the Dark Ages.

There are many well-known tales relating to the deeds of those spreading the word of God throughout the world, but the story below offers, what I feel to be, a good representation of how the heathens frequently saw their old ways undermined and destroyed.

29

# Nornagest

In Denmark there were many kings and queens who were wise or wicked, kind or greedy — but this story starts with a King and Queen who were wise and kind in ways that would even surprise us today in our modern times.

Through the wise counsel of each other, and the 'moots', or meetings with the local elders, this King and Queen were able to guide their peoples through a lifetime of peace and plenty.

They had one ever-so-common problem, however. They had no children, and this was something that plagued them until they were old.

Every day, for years, the otherwise happy King and Queen would ask themselves, and each other: "Why can we not have children? Why have the gods not granted us this blessing?" But they were wrong to worry so, for when they were both quite old they had a son.

You can imagine how excited everyone was. The King and Queen had their child and the people had their Prince, someone that they hoped would rule their kingdom as kindly as his fair parents. Everyone decided that this was to be no ordinary birth, and that there was to be a great feast. Soon the whole of Denmark was rushing around getting ready for the biggest celebration of their lifetime.

But the news did not stop there, and word of the great feast managed to make its way not only overseas, but to the root of Yggdrasil, the world tree itself, and to the three all-powerful Norns. They decided that they also would come to see this great prince.

So, when the child was born, everybody rushed to the castle and the feast began. The festivities seemed to be great success, and everybody commented upon how beautiful the baby was, and how delighted the old couple looked.

It is, as you well know, awfully bad luck to come to see a child and not bear gifts. So, everybody queued up with gifts to have a peek at the baby, and it was when this was happening that their surprise visitors arrived.

Urd, Nerthandr, and Skold came into the hall. This, everybody

31

said, must be a *very* special birthday.

First Urd, the Norn of the Past came up. She looked old and frail, but kind and wise, although some say she walked backwards.

"Oh, what a lovely baby," she cooed.

"I will give him the wisdom of the past. He shall know the fairest songs of the gods themselves and wisdom beyond his years."

Everyone clapped and said what a wonderful idea this was.

Next Nerthandr came up close; she looked like 'super-mum', attractive but also matronly and kind.

"He's a bonny lad," she said. "But bonnier yet, I'll have him, with good looks and health, and a voice like a skylark, he'll shine on all that see him."

Now everyone was getting really excited. One of the ladies present, in a fit of glee ran up to have another peek, to see what all this magic had done so far.

What a mistake, because she sent the final Norn, Skold, tumbling to the floor.

Now, you wouldn't call Skold a 'wicked witch', even if you weren't scared of her. She looked like a pretty adolescent girl and in part, even seemed benevolent — but did she ever have a temper!

Of the three Norns, it was Skold who controlled the future.

Without thinking she turned and spat out: "The gift I bring is his death." And then brushing the dust from her hooded dress, she pointed at a candle somewhere nearby, and said: "When that candle is done, so is that baby."

At this point, Skold remembered where she was, and that death was, if nothing else, a rather unorthodox birthday present.

She ran out with Urd following behind her.

Nerthandr, however, quietly took the candle and went up to the now devastated couple, saying: "Fear not, friends, this can be a blessing too. Keep this candle unlit, and whilst it never burns, his life will never fade,". She then gave the candle to the queen and left.

So, everything seemed all right, and the King and Queen could relax. However, they decided to call their son Nornagest, which means 'given blessings by the Norns', just to be on the safe side.

Nornagest grew up well, and was every bit as wise, good-looking, and alive as the Norns had told, but you can imagine that he was not your run-of-the-mill Prince. He also showed no interest in becoming King.

So when the King was ready to pass his throne on, it did not go to

Nornagest, but to a cousin or an uncle.

This was agreed to be the best thing, and Nornagest was allowed to follow his true calling, which was as a bard. This he did with splendour, entrancing and enchanting adults and children alike as he travelled from town to town with his tales and songs of the gods and their heroes.

Time went on and Nornagest did not age a day past his twenties, and all over Denmark, he was awaited eagerly until . . .

. . . a new King came with a new god.

King Olaf had been converted to the ways of a new god and didn't take kindly to people who still lived in the old ways. He had decided that the people of Denmark were to be baptised in the name of Jesus, and if they were unwilling, they, and their families were to be baptised in fire.

Soon people were less eager to hear the old songs of Nornagest, and where he once would have seen welcoming faces, he now saw shut doors and smouldering ruins.

Eventually King Olaf heard of this travelling blasphemous poet, and had him chased and arrested. Nornagest was brought to the halls of King Olaf, where the king demanded he entertain his host. Nornagest began playing his old songs of Odin, but Olaf was displeased.

"Enough of these pagan lies, bard, let us hear you sing of the joys of Jesus and our good Lord above."

"But these are the songs I know, my lord", answered Nornagest.

Enraged, the King turned to him, and yelled: "Then let us hear how well you can play you harp with no fingers."

Nornagest took the hint and started to improvise some songs with a more Christian feel. But brilliant as he was, the effect was not quite as sincere as he may have desired, and the atmosphere may not have seemed particularly elevated.

Then the King remembered the 'silly superstition' about Nornagest's candle.

"Let's have some more light in here!" boomed King Olaf. "Nornagest, you've got a candle, haven't you? Now why don't you light it?"

Nornagest resigned himself, and took his candle out, it was lit, and he returned to playing his music.

Beautiful, this music was, and it lasted for hours, getting ever fainter as the candle neared its end, until almost unnoticeably the songs, the candle, and Nornagest's life faded and blinked out forever.

# The Darkest Hour

*"Brother shall strike brother and both fall,*
*Sisters' sons defiled with incest;*
*Evil be on earth, an age of. Whoredom,*
*Of sharp sword-play and shields clashing,*
*A wind-age, a wolf-age till the world ruins:*
*No man to another shall mercy show."*

This excerpt from Voluspa or The Words of the Sybil is taken from W.H. Auden's translations from The Poetic Edda, or Codex Regis, and is meant to outline the time of Ragnarök — the Norse equivalent of Christian Armageddon.

However, it could be used easily to describe the immense evil and suffering of the two World Wars that spread from the then troubled lands of Germany.

Sadly, this dark episode strongly features the runes in a poor light, but for the sake of honesty, it cannot be omitted. If I could erase history, this period would be the first to go, but into it we must go with more detail than I would like to provide. Get ready for a re-rendition of a fairly grim tale that is not likely to endear you to the runes, but know that this is as bad at it gets.

At the close of the Middle Ages, several factors had opened up a new level of free discourse in Europe. Industrialism created a burgeoning middle classes with more time on their hands to think. In tandem, new liberal philosophies helped to shake off many oppressive thought structures of the past. Along with the sciences, the Romantic Movement emerged; a way of thinking that sought to revise our understanding of both nature and our ancient past.

Romanticism was in many important ways a good concept, allowing society to re-discover the lost wisdom and beauty of ancient culture generally. It eventually paved the way to a better understanding of non-western cultures, yet this new thinking had its darker side. Some people saw these connections to the past as justification for ideas of ethnic or national superiority, even though many others saw connectedness and liberality as the new underlying truth.

Things also got bigger - our houses, our cities, and our wars.

By the late 19th century, many European countries were involved in the building of empires, with their accumulated wealth largely based on the enforced poverty and enslavement of other peoples. The power that these countries amassed deeply destabilised Europe, creating a general undercurrent of distrust.

Ultimately, the whole of Europe was drawn into World War 1 when Germany, threatening France and breaking treaties with other countries including Britain and Russia, invaded Belgium. At this point, Germany's ruler Kaiser Wilhelm III modelled himself and his people after the Romans, and was attempting to emulate the Roman Empire (hence the epithet Caesar, or 'Kaiser' in German). This 'world war' led to a suffering and devastation that defied anything that people thought was possible at the time.

In 1918, at the war's end, the international community was devastated by what had been a war like no other. As a result, when Germany surrendered, it was punished harshly, throwing the already shattered nation into deep poverty.

Several years later, we were all to pay the price for this. Using bitterness among the German peoples, and a long-needed promise of salvation, Hitler, and his Nazi party were able to worm themselves into power.

The Nazis started with the promise of a new stronger Germany, but very soon returned to the vision of empire building. They also quickly started doing what they considered as a 'clean-up' of humanity. They believed, or wanted to believe, that they were initiating a new era in European history. But to this aim, they set about eliminating various groups of people — primarily the Jewish people, but also gays, disabled people, Gypsies, Slavs, and many others that they considered 'degenerate'.

To justify these appalling acts, they promoted the idea of a new Germanic 'Master Race' as based on one theory that all civilisations had arisen from 'Thule', a mythological northern equivalent of Atlantis. In this way, they were able to hitch themselves onto sentiments already present in the Romantic era.

Additionally, it is amusing to think that the myth of Thule is from Ancient Greek legend and not from the Norse or Germanic peoples; ironic also, that these Classical progenitors of the myth dubbed said northern types as 'Barbarians', which translates as "babblers".

As part of their propaganda, the Nazis added the Runes to their visual identity. They combined runic imagery with ancient Teutonic stories and Arthurian Legend among other things to reinvent history in their own chosen form - a history that placed their 'Aryan' people as superior to all others. This alleged superiority became the main sanction for their dark deeds.

They even chose to reinvent the Runes themselves, to some extent. Their own 'retro' version, dubbed 'Armenan' runes, based on the Younger Futhark. It was these runes that were touted as their ancient Aryan script.

The Nazis also used the Swastika, or ancient sun-wheel, which they chose as the symbol of their identity. The Swastika can be connected to the runes due to being found all over Europe, spanning right through prehistory. However, the Swastika is present fairly evenly on a global scale. Famously, it is still important in India, where it represents the Hindu god Ganesha. In keeping with their style, the Nazis altered this as well, spinning it the wrong way round. This was a strange choice. It means nothing happy, even for the wicked, arranged thus.

In truth, there were elements from many cultures that the Nazis used to further their ends, which they often later abandoned as it suited them. Roman eagles and Greek architecture were borrowed.

37

Hitler himself loved the legend of King Arthur and even had a Round Table commissioned. From an external viewpoint, it could be said that anything they could squeeze into their worrying ideologies without too much work went in. They even allegedly attempted Kabbalistic (Hebrew) magic, but it was the Runes that they blatantly plastered on vehicles, uniforms, etc.

As far as I'm concerned, the Runes backfired for the Nazis perfectly well. If you try to use runic magic to do bad things — you will get burned!

That said, the reputation of the Runes was tarnished by this incorrect use, and there are still many racists who choose runic emblems and the Swastika as their totems.

Unfortunately, this is encouraged by the somewhat overstated macho image of the warrior Vikings, which still seems to appeal to Europe's far-right. Many of these extremists still put themselves forward as this dreadful 'Master race', with the Runes and Vikings as part of their chosen (dubious) proof of their superiority just as the Nazis did. All of this despite the ever-present, but continuously growing masses of archaeological, anthropological, and geographical evidence that refutes them.

Archaeology and ancient records, including those of Norse and Saxon peoples, point to a surprisingly large amount of movement and mixture amongst early humans, making the most painfully isolated amongst us remarkably racially mixed. For example, Sumerian, Ancient Egyptian, and Classical culture all only survived as long as they did because of adoption by several sets of new people, and some of these people were originally either foreign invaders or slaves. In fact 'racially mixed' doesn't really go far enough, with recent discoveries regarding Neanderthal genetics proving that we are not even solely the product of one species, let alone breed. If we are not all equal, then none of us are equal.

Now we have trawled the darkest aspect to the history of the Runes, and dark it is, but let us move on. Like almost any religion, science or philosophy, the runes can and have been involved in catastrophe and cruelty, but in equal measure they can be used for kindness and benefit. Maybe more worryingly, they can also do all of these accidentally. Good and evil may seem apparent externally, but internally they are not always neon lit. The Runes can be used for good or ill, but in fairness so can your mouth, your hands, and your feet. Caution is a prerequisite with anything exciting, and plenty of things that appear quite boring.

Maybe the good news is that if this sorry episode hasn't got you running to the hills, it is unlikely that anything else in this book will. This unwanted legacy troubles many genuine rune practitioners, as perhaps it should, but I hope that you will see the Runes and what they have to offer as both more and better than this.

# The New Dawn

After what can only be called a bad millennium for the runes, attitudes are beginning to change. An almost worldwide disillusionment with modernism, Christianity, and the promise of a bright technological future has begun to let mysticism of many types back in.

In fact, all varieties of ancient cultures have enjoyed all varieties of revival. Presently, there are plenty of shops in most towns selling books and objects relating to Buddhism, Druidism or Wicca, Shamanism, and of course, the Runes.

The Runes benefited from their inclusion in the works of J.R.R Tolkien, who used his stories to promote a simpler rural existence, in place of industrialisation.

This is a more positive and realer association for the Runes and has brought many of the right people back in touch with the true call of their nature. Indeed, many Rune users recommend *The Lord of the Rings* as a first stop, despite the fact that Tolkien was an avid Christian.

People also wear runic talismans and charms as symbols of peace and the desire to live in closer touch with the natural world.

This is a true new dawn for the Runes — not as the symbol of world leaders and empire builders, but as the symbol of honest people who see themselves as citizens of the earth and not its rulers.

# Digging up the Runes

In this present age, what remains are only clues as to how the Runes were originally used for magical purposes. This is mainly because the aforementioned spread of monotheism throughout Europe during the Dark and Middle Ages, which brought with it an intolerance of the older faiths.

During this time much was destroyed, including temples, statues, and holy artefacts. Even the memory of Paganism was destroyed where it could be.

There was also reluctance on the part of the holy peoples of Europe to write down their beliefs. This was in part due to the belief that writing made people lazy with regards to the learning of important information.

Even what we know is from medieval scripts of varying reliability. The scholars who wrote these scripts were mostly Christians and it is likely that they have tampered with the material, either to promote their Christian ideas or scandalise the heathen ones. We also have archaeological finds, albeit not many.

Other hints we have concerning how the Runes were used for magic come from the detailed records made by the Romans during their military campaigns in Northern Europe — Germanica by Tacitus, and Julius Caesar's The Conquest of Gaul, to name but two. We need to take these with a pinch of salt, though. Certain inaccuracies (such as their description of elks as having no knees, and oxen with three horns) point either to them having romanticised their campaigns with fiction, or the locals 'taking the piss' with their tall stories.

Another well-used source is folklore.

However, one problem with folklore is that after the near-universal demise of the oral tradition in the western world, many stories and chants are lost, and, yet again, what material has survived has often been romanticised and distorted by those that shared them.

To make matters worse, ironically, as literacy grew, written and altered folk tales re-entered the consciousness of the people, frequently ousting or distorting the original material.

For proof of this dire status think Cinderella. We all know Cinderella don't we? Actually Cinderella has several versions, one even in the Hebrides of Scotland where she is a male 'Jack' like character named 'Assipattle', or 'paddles in ashes'. Even Dick Whittington may actually be a 'Cinderella' relic. Part of a whole family of rags to riches tales. Or maybe it's just a common human theme, we can't tell. What most of us have is Disney's rehash of Jacob Grimm's albeit accurate rendering of only one German version. Rumplestiltskin, alike, was a small black imp with a swishy tail in the South of England, and Nornagest (later described) sounds like he either borrowed or leant a wicked baptism gift with The Sleeping beauty. Volund the smith was also 'Wayland' in the UK, which is truer?

Add to this the need or desire of modern occultists to attach their modern understandings to their foggy ancient past, and you begin to get the picture.

An interesting example is the Celtic script, Ogham, which is now being used in a similar way to the Runes. That you can use Ogham for divination I have no doubt of, but to suggest that it was done at the time is highly questionable. Ogham has only ever been found on stone monuments. There are no recorded allusions to Ogham being used for divination. To my knowledge, it was used solely to represent the phonetic values of words and names. They are invariably marks on a continuous line, and not throwable icons. Is this new use spiritual, meaningful, and potent? Probably, yes. Are you doing what the Druids, or indeed any Celt ever did? I have my doubts.

However, the Vikings were luckily loud, violent, and formidable enough to leave a moderately decent amount of resources for the studious to learn from, or at least enough to get started.

Graffiti in Maes Howe, a Neolithic cairn in Orkney, tells us not just what Brian Blood-Axe thought of the local ladies, but also what his friends believed to be the complete set of Runes, as they wrote the Futhark down (misspelled, some argue).

Unlike many ancient alphabets (Hebrew, Cuneiform, Ancient Egyptian), the Runes use vowels. This makes it easier for archaeologists to discover whether inscriptions were intended for reading.

In this wise, many runic finds remain that were almost definitely intended for magical or symbolic uses. These magical runes are found on weapons, tools, calendars (almanacs), houses and monuments all over Europe and date from Pre Christian times to around the 19th century in some remote areas of Eastern Europe.

Also, written poems that have survived, albeit in their tampered forms. They are at least known to have been written within living memory of the Pagan times when the Runes were widely used. Norse Poems, such as *Voluspa*, *Havamal*, and *Sigdrifumal*, recorded by Snorri Sturluson in the 11th Century and the earlier *Codex Regis* (Latin for 'book of kings' also known as the Poetic, or *Elder Edda*) illustrate that they were used for spells, chants, and talismans, and even provide hints as to their uses.

We also have three medieval texts describing the Runes themselves directly. There are two medieval rune poems from Norway, and Iceland, and then we have the oldest, the *Anglo-Saxon Rune Poem*.

So while we may have an incomplete picture of the Runes, we still have plenty to work with.

# Are the Runes for you?

## *An Ancient System for Modern Truths?*

"Why have I just bought a book on some freaky weird philosophy that, for all I know, should have been ditched along with flint spears and axes?"

This may well be a question you're asking yourself right now, or maybe you're not as cynical as I frequently am, when introduced to yet another alternative science or self-help method.

So, what will this book do for you?

Will it make you rich?

Will it improve your sex-life?

Will it have you spinning off into psychedelic worlds?

Will it make you a better person?

The answer to these questions is "Well… Maybe." If the simple action of reading a book, any book, can reliably do this for you please get in touch. I want a copy.

Will knowledge of the Runes make you a cut above the rest? Absolutely not!

However, what this book offers is a system of magic and belief that could well change your life forever. This is a kick-start to understanding the Runes, which, in my opinion is one of the most beautiful, exciting, and potent systems around. There are exciting experiences on the way too. The Runes offer us an understanding of existence that the people of the Western world have sadly neglected for well over a millennium — if not longer.

The Runes explain the landscape of life in colour, with every living experience being crammed with spirit, portent, and purpose, as well as humour. They embody the spirit of being, as seen by the ancient peoples of the Northern Hemisphere and beyond.

## *Are you right for the runes?*

You may also be wondering whether you're qualified to use the Runes.

You may or may not be the kind of person who already feels particularly in touch with the spirit world at this time.

Whether someone is a spiritually wise or good person will always be guesswork, and whether the Runes are to play a large role in your life is also a question that can only be answered personally.

Some people claim their right to be seen as 'mystical' by pointing to their descent from a mystical family, or will claim to have been 'chosen', somehow. Within their context, maybe there is a grain of truth, but while many mystical systems were possibly created for and by a mystical elite, the Runes were not. Legend and record make it clear that they are learned, and not inherited.

Part of the reason why the Runes have survived intact is that from the heart of Russia to the shores of Iceland and throughout the entire of Europe, they were used by kings, farmers, holy-men, tramps ('hermits'), fishermen and toilet cleaners alike.

You do not therefore need be born into the runes or even initiated into them.

The Runes were also used equally by men and women. When picturing the society of the Runes, it is hard not to get bogged down with the images of 'manly' Vikings wielding their swords and supping their ales in between their raping and pillaging. As you read on it will become apparent that this is a gross simplification of even the men in this culture, but it would be brazen follly to say that the Runes were not for women too.

Much of the importance of women and their goddesses has now been lost because most of the characters who bothered, or were allowed, to write down the Viking sagas and rune poems were wealthy Christian men. It also didn't help that medieval Christianity was no fan of mystical or wise Pagan women.

Having said all of this, the roles of women in rune lore are more screamed than whispered. One of the most famous pieces of Viking literature is called '*Voluspa*', which translates as 'What the Volva said'. The word Volva has gradually been corrupted in modern society to mean the vagina, but originally was the name for a wise woman. The Volva were the women who devoted their lives to spirituality, and they were more than regarded highly. Often these women were consulted before preparing for battle or when crops were failing, as they were thought to be particularly fine-tuned into the spirit world. For those interested, this practice is mentioned in *The Saga of Erik the Red*.

Freya Aswynn, in her acclaimed book *Magic and Mysteries in the Northern Tradition* has suggested that the word Anglo Saxon word 'cunt' may be connected in origin to the word 'cunning', maybe underlying its true meaning — 'wise like a lady'.

In Laukassanna, Loki, the principal deity of evil, accuses Odin himself of dressing up as a lady and doing 'sidr' or 'woman magic'. This is an accusation that most scholars believe to be taken as true.

The Freya cult, worshippers of the goddess Freya, were one of the last Pagan bastions to fall in Europe. This was probably because the women involved would have had to give up much of their traditional power and respect, were they to adhere with the patriarchal ways of Christianity. However, long after Christianity had pretty much wiped out Heathenism among the male population, there really were witches, dancing in the moonlight.

On the other hand, men are magical too.

One feature the Runes has in common with many of the truly ancient cultures is a total disobedience to the idea of gender archetypes. There are certainly overtly 'feminine' goddesses and overtly 'masculine' gods, but at the same time there is plenty in between. One thing that I am keen to remind people is that the god of beauty, music, and poetry is indeed a god, and that the goddess Freya is not someone you'd wisely anger.

This might sound strange, but I genuinely suspect that humanity has never been more ignorant about the sexes. Dividing aggression and gentleness as gender divisions, and even colour coding toys pink and blue are worrying traits.

In nature and spirit, we are perhaps more well-rounded than we think, with much of our currently gender aligned instincts present wherever they are needed and not doled out by our crotches.

Remember that working with polarity may be something of a convenient shortcut, although that polarity might not always be relevant to the truth.

For a start, it is much easier to treat someone badly if you both believe that you have different abilities and weaknesses. In this way, differentiation is very convenient for many people of both sexes.

The rune Mann ( ᛗ ) depicting the full human race, both male and female bothers neither with the depiction of the phallus, nor the vagina — two images that the Teutonic peoples and the Vikings were not afraid to use. Personally, I read this symbol as a hint that, spiritually at least, the differences between male and female are mostly those which we concoct for ourselves.

Other than the obvious physical gender-specific traits, nobody really knows how different males are to females - but we are more than sure that your gender needn't alter your abilities to use strength, intuition, logic, empathy, receptivity, and the other gamut of mental persuasions.

The Runes need males and females alike, and your path will be chosen due to your real personal abilities.

We are all wise beings to some extent, and where intelligence, ability, and morality may vary, they vary from person to person and not sex to sex, race to race or in any other orderly fashion whatsoever.

Like any other skills, the Runes require patience and a good deal of time to master to any great level. There are people who have spent their whole lives dedicated to understanding the Runes, and who will still argue that they don't know half of what's there.

## *On to the Harder Part*

If you are still contemplating the pros and cons of the Runes and investigating what they are all about, it is hard to ignore their past connections with racism, as you will certainly come up against it.

Elitism is rife in mystical circles but the Runes particularly have suffered here.

Please do not let this put you off the Runes, as the Runes are not racist themselves.

Modern research into Teutonic settlements now hints at these northern and Germanic peoples being far more cosmopolitan than many of their contemporaries, having Roman, Slavic, and Asian peoples living freely in many of their capital cities. In these settlements, many cultures and religions seem to have been allowed to co-exist in equity. The Roman historian Tacitus actually notes this in his reports.

The Vikings themselves are slightly less easy to understand, as they were never really what you could call a regulated society, but on the whole they seem about as good or bad as anyone else during that particular era. Looking at the Viking gods themselves - they obviously had a hell of a lot more time for the disabled than Romans, Celts or early Christians who generally burned those deemed not quite up to scratch.

One Viking king did claim to have a dream where he was told that his heirs would be the people that ruled the world, but trust me there are a whole load of kings of many shapes, colours, and sizes that have tried that routine.

Many Vikings also believed that the spoils of war could include slaves. This was where society was at worldwide at the time and it wasn't a race thing. Vikings made slaves of fellow Vikings as readily as anyone else. Strangely, the Viking nation of Iceland was the first nation on Earth to ban slavery.

I would personally argue that the Romans and Francs were the true advocates of racism and imperialism in these eras, two things that the Teutonic peoples originally fought tooth and nail against. It was largely with the coming of early Christianity that the people of the North started playing 'I am better than you' styled games.

If the connection with racism troubles you as much as it troubles me, bear in mind that many of the Runes are believed to have descended from pre-runic symbols that have been found worldwide, dating back further than man's migration from Africa, let alone some 19th Century fool's ideas about alleged European superiority.

Many gay people now wear runic emblems and the other

symbols relating to right-wing movements just to annoy the right-wing contingent in our society, and I must say that my hat goes off to them.

I hope in the meantime to present the Runes as they really are and always were: class-less, race-less and elite-less.

This book aims to bring the Runes back to the people — everyone in fact who wants them.

Whether the Runes are a system that you should use exclusively is up to you. I cannot answer that. The important thing is that, unlike many other systems, they are open to anyone.

To many people the Runes are simply an ancient European text, but to those who use them for magic and wisdom, they are much more than that. They spread back to before mankind existed, let alone our foolish social divides. If the Runes are racist, then cows are the master race, as you will soon find out.

What I hope in the meantime is that you will see that, traditionally speaking, there is no set of qualifications needed to find the Runes useful.

So, if you're sitting there thinking, "I'm obviously not European, what have the Runes got for me?", my answer is heaps. Indeed, the devil in me says, "Welcome brave warrior, you shall teach as much as you shall learn".

Odin himself was not natively connected to the runes, he had to seek them and learn.

# How do the Runes Work?

This may sound obvious, but is important to know what you believe about what you're doing, and what you believe that you are going to attain by doing it. Having your own standpoint as the basis of your methodology will help you greatly. Of course, how any mystical system really works is not an easy question, and book-to-book you will find an overwhelming list of theories and conjectures.

Like almost everybody else, I have my own set of opinions as to the inner workings of the Runes and their efficacy. This will be revealed, I but also feel that it would be best to try and provide a couple of the more popular theories, along with a few issues that may need to be considered when trying to use the Runes.

## *The Subconscious Mind*

There has been a tendency among modern thinkers to offer up the subconscious as a kind of free ticket to the spirit world, but one issue that is rarely dealt with in fortune telling and mystical literature is exactly where the subconscious ends and the mystical truth begins. This has important connotations for the mystic.

Knowing that this previous statement provides quite a lot to chew on, I'll explain myself:

Firstly, what is the subconscious?

The subconscious is the name given to the parts of your mind that you are unaware of on a day to day basis, regulating a wide range of mental functions that vary from simple things like walking without thinking and pulling away from pain, to controlling what we remember and when, as well as dreams. This is a vast subject about which little is still known, and many exciting experiments have been conducted to see just what is in this elusive and vast portion of our minds.

The subconscious mind seems to contain far more information than we can easily understand; under a state of hypnosis, many people have been able to relate experiences long forgotten, and even sometimes discover skills that they didn't know that they had. Under similar conditions, many people have claimed to have had past life memories brought out or to be able to see things from distant times and places. It is common therefore for people to explain the use of mystical systems to tap into spiritual or esoteric (secret) knowledge basing their assertions on one of the following ideas.

- Your subconscious mind is a marvellous wandering beast that roams the spirit-world with ease (that is to say, it is your unrestrained soul), and by communicating directly with it, you can discover your true spiritual identity and destiny.

- All things are part of one system, and so the subconscious can merely stick a proverbial spitty finger out and feel the wind of the spirit world.

- Your subconscious mind secretly holds all of the thoughts of your ancestors down to the beginning of time, and with this almost infinite experience it is almost infinitely wise.

- Conversely, maybe your subconscious mind isn't at all spiritually wise, but contains enough information from your life to be a hell of a lot better at calculating things than you are.

Now, any or many of these statements could be true and I've heard all of them being explained, very poetically, as the working system behind a variety of occult systems, including the Runes.

However, all these ideas pose some difficult questions.

Firstly, the subconscious mind has been revealed to be as human as the parts of the mind that we do know about. To be specific, the subconscious mind can lie, it frequently doesn't know answers to esoteric questions, and in the state of hypnosis, it can actually unwittingly invent memories of both childhood experiences and past lives that can be proven categorically wrong.

In short, the subconscious is just as imaginative as it is observant or spiritual.

There is also the issue of whether the subconscious will be able at first glance to understand the Runes any better than you can – because, let's face it, they do at least initially just look like a bunch of lines, no matter how wonderful we believe them to be.

To drill down into this a little, how might we know that your subconscious mind is going to pick out the rune Thorn ( ᚦ ) because it's 'Thorn' — and not just because, "It's the nice one with the little triangle on a stick."

I personally find it hard to work with the theory that the subconscious mind, which is so elusive in day to day life, happens to be fluent in the languages and ideologies of Hebrew, I-Ching, the Tarot and the Runes. If it is, then why can't I play the trumpet?

Also, it's hard to believe that archetypes — even if your subconscious is able to perceive them in such abstract systems — will be read similarly from person to person.

For instance, let us take an apparently straight forward archetype like 'the father'.

If a symbol of the father appears to someone who was abused by their father as a child then its meaning could share little in common with the same symbol for an individual whose father was contrastingly pleasant.

Likewise, imagine getting a horse in your reading.

If you are constantly having nightmares about horses rearing up and stamping on you, then your interpretation will be different from that of an avid horse rider.

This points to the idea that, if your use of the Runes is going to be based on the subconscious, then you may have to make some fairly fundamental decisions about how to employ them, particularly when it comes to using them as an oracle, or fortune telling system.

You will have to decide whether or not making readings with people untrained in the Runes is a valid form of divination, or whether only the person who is trained in runic lore will be able to subconsciously choose the right runes for the questioner.

You will also have to decide whether you or the untrained viewer will need to be questioned about the imagery, and whether or not they have particularly strong or unusual feelings towards the symbols presented. Maybe the presence of Yr ( ᛦ ), the Yew Tree rune, means "Yes, you should be a gardener."

With regards to magic and meditation, you are also going to have to get to know the Runes on an expertly academic level, as well as asking yourself, for instance, how well you are going to be able to relate to 'Ur' ( ᚢ ) which symbolises an extinct relative of the cow or buffalo — unless of course you believe that you have experienced this extinct animal as part of the collective unconscious.

After saying this, I do not want to completely dismiss the role of the subconscious mind as a tool to tap into spiritual or even better mental abilities. But if you do believe that the Runes are a way to communicate with your subconscious, make sure your subconscious is given a chance to actually work with the Runes themselves, and that you and it are not just guessing.

## *The Dice Man*

There have always been people who have used ancient oracular systems without actually genuinely believing that there is any spiritual or subconscious links to deep truths at all, and whilst I am not one of them, I feel that their reasons for using the Runes are still valid.

I have titled this category of belief in oracles (if you can call it that) 'The Dice Man' after a famous book by an American author named Luke Reinhart, in which a man decides to live out his life by making decisions using a die.

In brief, the idea is that no information is bad information insofar as you may actually receive ideas that you would not have otherwise guessed, and thus be able to take on a new perspective.

In this way, you can actually gain useful information without having to believe in the system — you are merely using it as a second opinion, and can discard their suggestions or use them to add new perspectives to a given situation or question.

Thus, what the Runes provide for the non-believer is a ready-made system for generating or stimulating ideas that is simple and convenient to use — no yarrow sticks, calculators, or even paper and pen are needed — and their meanings can be taken as they are.

There are also the benefits to be had in learning to work with abstract concepts and creating complex ideas and arguments from them, as well as the development of improvisational skills that may be deemed useful.

Of course, the magical side of the Runes — dealt with later on in this book — does require belief, and where gods or spirits are referred to, these will have to be used at least as metaphors.

So, you can only go so far with the Runes merely acting on such a mundane level. However, a lot of rune readers start here as it's quite hard for a rational and intelligent human being to tell their rational and intelligent friends: "Oh, by the way, I believe that God was licked out of a bloody great pile of salt by a giant cow." To add to this, if you are beginning in the Runes, then simply being curious is probably the best state of mind.

## God or Spirit Power

This theory states that it is not your subconscious mind, or even particularly your own spirit, that is controlling the Runes, but it is the Runes themselves. This is maybe the hardest theory to work with for many — but is the one that I go by myself.

For this to work successfully your subconscious does need to be keyed in - but this is just so you can empower the Runes with your own energies, and thus convert them from strange abstract shapes or objects into working Runes, much in the same way that electricity and impulse signals convert a grey box with glass in the front of it into a television.

Under the surface, the Runes are indeed picking up on your feelings and circumstances and reflecting these, but it is the Runes themselves, as divine energies, that are being presented.

In such readings, you needn't worry about who chooses the Runes as the Runes will hopefully be choosing themselves, and whilst you may choose to use a questioner's personal feelings towards the symbols, the traditional or authentic Rune meanings can also be taken as they stand.

There are many legends asserting the power of the Runes to break chains, to save the dying, to transform, to create and to destroy and these rumours have persisted from the days of Julius Caesar right up to the present day. If you believe in the magical powers of the Runes, then you will probably also find the magical practices in this book a rewarding set of experiences.

Don't expect miracles — or at least don't expect overnight ones. This is a book for beginners and novices. However, with this book as a starting point, you should find that the experiences and effects that the Runes have will grow with your ability to understand them as well as your readiness to shoulder the responsibility.

Yes, I really do believe that the Runes were discovered by a god called Odin, whilst hanging upside down from the tree of life, or Yggdrasil as it was called in Norse, and also that like Odin, you can journey in this quest for truth — although you may or may not find it necessary to hang upside down in a tree, and hopefully you won't be eaten by a wolf.

There is a downside to this type of use of the Runes. Frequently, the Runes are as rewarding as the average attempt at levitation, in that if you aren't in a 'magical state', then the Runes usually won't play. No fairy dust — no flying!

You can add to this that whatever this fairy dust might be is questionable to the extent that it's barely reliable enough for a party trick, and elusive in the laboratory.

Here I venture to say that your subconscious is both your ally and your obstacle. Magic certainly works better when you're in another place, but subconscious thought is another 'self' that you maybe need to avoid, or get to know to the extent that you can dismiss it occasionally. The subconscious is frequently the part of you that gets stuck in routines, including destructive ones.

After a reading, a friend of mine once said something on the lines of: "I don't know whether we're getting the truth here, but we are definitely getting to what I really feel." As the product of a reading from stick-shaped marks, that's a pretty interesting state to be in: uncanny and useful in itself, but not ideal. I consider this tendency to be the biggest stumbling block of fortune telling in general. Once you get past the conscious part of you that can definitely lie to itself, as well as being wrong, you still have the subconscious.

What you are aiming for, in my opinion, is something that is not yourself at all.

Most practitioners would argue, as I would, that their chosen method of divination is reliable enough to be informative and compelling, and that is where I stand. While it is good enough to amaze you, it will still not be time to throw away the newspaper, and nor will it have you hovering along the pavement on your way to work.

# The Runes and other Mystical Systems

The Runes are just one magical system among many. Many other systems have far larger groups of practitioners, or even holy orders. Whilst these groups are likely of varying levels of sincerity and import, knowing about these other systems may be useful to you.

Some of these orders and societies are in constant contact or conflict with each other, and many people drift from group to group, learning and choosing from parts of a mixture of faiths and societies. This has good points and bad points.

These societies are nearly all actively engaged in learning more and it is certainly true that these communities can serve the mystic well. The challenges and discourse of others keep the mind open, and a support network is also good for when one gets stuck. Certainly, Odin himself had no qualms about going to the most dubious sources (dwarves, giants, and the land of the dead) for information. Any knowledge is good knowledge. Surely there is no such thing as a belief that has nothing to learn from.

However, there are drawbacks.

Be careful, for example, when mixing and matching the Runes with eastern philosophies, Wicca, or those of monotheistic faiths such as Christianity, Islam and Zoroastrianism. While these can be useful as metaphors, they can also be misleading.

Many people have attempted to link the Runes with other religions or codes of mystical practice, and this is tempting when real runic practises are hard to research — but this combining of ideologies can make true understanding of the Runes difficult.

The Runes have similarities with other systems — particularly the Qabalah, the Hebrew alphabet that also claims to represent the elements of the universe. They are, however, not identical, and many parallels that are drawn between the Runes and other systems are at best forced and sometimes plain wrong.

Trying to form meaningful direct correspondences between all of the Runes and the Qabalah will be a struggle, and possibly a waste of time. Neither do the Runes relate to the popular teachings of Aleister Crowley nor the Golden Dawn. And neither are they Buddhist.

For instance, there are hints in some Viking texts at there being a universal creator god, but it would not be recognisable in any standard monotheistic terms. The presence that willed the creation of the universe is not thought of in the normal terms of an emotional being, such as a human or animal, and neither is it seen as friend nor foe of order, chaos, good or evil.

Likewise, the Odinic gods that are human or at least anthropomorphic are not likely to relate logically to any other system closely enough to be dependable. Odin is not Mercury, Jupiter, Lugh, Gabriel, Quetzocoatl, or any other god — he's just Odin.

This is not to say that there aren't connections between all faiths. Some ideas are obviously plain true, and if you believe that there is probably one mystic truth from which all mystical thoughts are derived, you're not alone. But lumping different cosmologies together should be done with caution. This is one of the best ways of diluting and thus losing information forever.

In other words, the Runes and the Norse gods are not there for us to pick-and-mix energies and deities, and then loosely patch them together for convenience.

# Are the Runes Dangerous?

*"Better not to ask than to over-pledge*
*As a gift that demands a gift*
*Better not to send than to slay too many."*

In Havamal, which is allegedly the words of Odin, the above warning is given. The short answer to the question, "are the runes dangerous?" is, "Yes" — but so is driving an automobile.

The Runes are not evil in any way, but there's no safety belt, and you can use them for harm as easily as you can use them for good.

I could sum up my warning by mentioning that the Anglo-Saxon rune for magic is 'Gar' — the double ended spear of Odin, which also embodies the rune of 'Gifu' ( X ) which can represent sacrifice.

You can perhaps understand from this analogy that any magic you do will have a rebound. Good begets good and likewise bad will beget bad.

The other thing I should mention is that mystical understanding, despite what many personal growth books suggest, is no easier than the more conventional choices of Christianity or Atheism.

The world of the Runes is still a place where every action is accountable, and many things do not go the way you'd like. The Runes are not a get out of jail free card.

While any enlightenment is always a good thing, you cannot expect the truth or any expression of it to put an endless grin of delight upon your face. Odin himself, the patron of the Runes, is allegedly eternally troubled by some of the absolute truths he attained.

Neither are the Runes an escape route from reality to a better place. Many people try to use them like this, but this is not their purpose, and any experiences you gain by using the Runes should not be used as a replacement for living in the real word— fundamentally because this type of escape is not good for you.

Whatever we were put on this earth for, it wasn't just to buzz off back into the spirit world, or simply have our own way from birth to death. The delights and the anguish of this world are here specifically for us to learn from and we are, at least to some extent, here for them.

Having said all of this, as long as you are willing to be responsible to some extent, and take the knocks with the caresses, the Runes offer a world of opportunity. You have a chance to understand, live, and work with the cosmos as the ancients once did — and that is not something that can be said of many practices in our daily lives today.

# The Meanings of the Runes

This chapter discusses meanings of the Runes with regards to their oracular and magical meanings, as well as their literal meanings.

I will mainly focus on the Elder Futhark, which is considered the oldest rune-set.

However, I'll also take the time to briefly cover the later Anglo-Saxon additions to this rune-set, but only because one of the main texts I'll be discussing in relation to the Futhark is the *Anglo-Saxon Rune Poem*. I do not use these extra Anglo-Saxon runes.

There are few authentic sources for Rune knowledge and many of them, including the *Anglo-Saxon Rune Poem*, are written in Christian times, and are swayed thus.

Other authentic ancient references that I've used to gather these descriptions are *Havamal* or *The Words of the Wise one*, which is a poem from the *Elder Edda,* and Snorri Sturlluson's *Edda*, both written some time between 1200 and 1241. These texts are not provided in this section for clarity.

You will also note that I make various references to gods and other mystical concepts throughout this section. They are also vital clues. While I hope that these concepts are explained clearly enough to make sense at the time, they are explained in greater depth in later chapters. Hopefully it will all make sense in the end.

There are a lot of questions as to the pronunciations of the various Runes, and their literal meanings. This may be related to their association with a lot of Vikings who spelt erratically as much as it relates to the various Futharks out there.

Many may claim to know, but I suspect they don't, and I recommend choosing the names that you prefer.

In the "Various Names" section of the table below I include, first, my preferred Anglo-Saxon name, and then the Germanic name — which is a particularly popular standard right now. The names following are just samples of other names I've come across from time to time.

While endeavouring to give you a few of the more common name choices, I cannot claim to have all of the suggested variants that I've come across, as I feel that this may prove more confusing than helpful.

Twenty years ago, when I first started learning the Runes, nearly all books referred to the Runes by similar names to those used by the Saxons, but nowadays, most rune authors rely more heavily on the old Germanic names.

These Germanic names are reconstructed, in that most of them are not currently to be found directly in archaeological records. They have been deduced by studying related languages in the same way that the Proto Indo European language has been reconstructed, using etymology. They have, however been reconstructed with enough academic rigour for this naming convention to be accepted by both mystics and historians alike, so it is not my place to go against them.

I do worry that a factor that might play a role in this change is that the simpler Anglo-Saxon names may just sound less mystical, or sophisticated. This is ironically part of the reason that I prefer them, as it makes the whole thing sound and feel less pompous to me.

If this conflict troubles you, allow me to reassure you that whilst their full names may differ from culture to culture, they do not vary so heavily with their written phonetic values, or even meanings.

In my opinion, their phonetic values are the sum of their spoken power, which is overridden in turn by their visual significance. Their full names in various cultures provide us with valuable clues to their full meanings. They also help them slide off the tongue a little easier, or sound cooler, but that they differ or that you prefer different variants is not something that I would lose sleep over.

When clarifying the phonetic values of the Runes, I have worked with the more debated runes by calculating what is actually needed to clarify written words and looking at similarities throughout their array of different names.

For instance, Eohll ( ᛉ ) is represented by most people nowadays as having a "zz" noise, but the Anglo-Saxon system has it as "Eohll", which is totally unrelated, and the "zz" noise could easily be created by doubling the Sig Rune.

The Latin alphabet is unusual in that it has some completely pointless letters, such as "X" for the "ks" noise and "Z" for the "ss" noise. I don't believe that the Elder Futhark shares this trait.

| | |
|---|---|
| **Feoh "f"** | **Yr "y" or "i"** |
| cattle, wealth | yew, turmoil, strength |
| **Ur "u"** | **Peorth "p"** |
| Auroch, buffalo | surprise, secret, mystery |
| **Thorn "th"** | **Eohll "ey"** |
| thorn, devil | declare, protect, beseech |
| **Ansur "a"** | **Sig "s"** |
| mouth, god | sun, victory, vanquish |
| **Rad "r"** | **Tyr "t"** |
| cyclic motion, travel | courage, decisions, honour |
| **Kaon "c"** | **Birca "b"** |
| torch, knowledge | mother, new life, planning |
| **Gyfu "g"** | **Eh "e"** |
| gift, meeting, kiss | horse, travel, companions |
| **Wunna "w"** | **Mann "m"** |
| happiness, contentment | mankind, society |
| **Hagal "h"** | **Lagu "l"** |
| hail, act of the gods | sea, emotions, life |
| **Niet "n"** | **Ing "ng"** |
| the knot, difficulties | source, creativity, new |
| **Iss "I"** | **Othel "o"** |
| eyes, ice, stasis | home, background |
| **Jera "j"** | **Dag "d"** |
| year, harvest | day, beginning, end |

# Various Names

The symbols also vary slightly between Rune practitioners in proportion and shape.

Ing ( ✖ ) is frequently drawn as a simple shape resembling the diamond symbol on a pack of cards.

This isn't contradictory, and visually represents the same motifs well. It still echoes creation in its many forms. However, the larger version resembling two "X" shapes helps to encourage the idea of inspiration coming from other worlds or spiritual spheres. Both forms are present in authentic historical records.

Ing also appears in mediaeval magical scripts as a string of "diamonds", suggesting an infinite shape of which both forms are adequate representations.

The variant of Jera ( ✧ ) shown in this book is quite unusual.

Jera is frequently shown in modern books as two Kaon runes encircling each other in a clockwise fashion, but here I have enclosed them to create a central diamond shape.

While there are others who use the version shown here, I feel I should explain that this is partly because many runic finds present the rune Jera as an enclosed Ing shape (again, like "diamonds" on a pack of cards) with a long line dividing it down the centre. I believe that it is beneficial to keep the presence of this Ing shape, which hints yet again at the shape of the world, the diagonals representing its continued cycle of time. What you get here is not the most common form, but the closest to the average, if that makes sense.

The rune Kaon ( ＜ ) is sometimes drawn similarly to the letter K with one of the diagonals removed.

There is also a rune variant named 'Kalc' or 'Kaun', which resembles the rune Eohll, only upside-down. I associate this rune form more with the Younger Futhark than the Elder Futhark which is the pivot of this book. It also appears as the letter 'r' if things weren't complicated enough.

Whilst it's interesting that the Younger Futhark gave the reverse of Eohll its own separate name, this does not aid us with deciphering Kaon itself. It does not share the traditional torch motif.

The rune Ansur ( ᚠ ) is sometimes switched for one of its closely related Anglo-Saxon equivalents, in either name or form. This is not a huge problem because the equivalent Anglo-Saxon rune means effectively the same thing.

# Freya's eight

## Feoh

ᚠ

*Wealth is a comfort to all men;*
*yet must every man bestow it freely*
*if he wish to gain honour in the sight of the Lord.*

Keywords: cows, wealth, status, sustenance, love, care

Feoh, first and foremost, represents one of mankind's greatest and oldest allies — the cow.

This may seem strange to the casual observer, but it is in fact the same even for the Greek and Latin alphabets, where aleph or alpha also represents the cow.

From pole to pole, cows are used as a source of milk, meat, clothing, and even cement for houses, and in early European pastoral society, if one had a lot of cows, one was considered wealthy.

Feoh is, therefore, the rune of moveable wealth, but also the wealth that you have to work with to keep. This is because cows, like many forms of wealth, need to be nourished, nurtured and protected - these responsibilities are also represented.

Cows were also greatly esteemed, and Norse Legend has it that the Gods of the universe themselves were created or released by a giant cow named Audhumla (the nourisher), who licked their forms out of a lump of salt.

In positive readings this rune can represent the coming of great comfort and prosperity through one's own effort.

It can also represent the status that comes with this wealth.

Likewise, Feoh can suggest the forming, or settling of a long living relationship, as people commit themselves to each other, and it appears in many love spells.

Feoh is a positive rune, and in an otherwise indifferent reading, Feoh offers the comforts of wealth, and/or a steady relationship. In fact, many rune books written around the 1970s and '80s had 'love' as its primary meaning, although this has gone out of fashion. This element of Feoh cannot be dismissed just because of modern notions of love that conflict with ideas of status and ownership. Love is a wealth of sorts, whether we like it or not — and it certainly requires a considerable amount of nurturing.

However, Feoh only ever represents the practical side of love, and if other emotional runes or outside factors are discouraging, then Feoh can be seen as a warning of responsibilities and a long uphill struggle.

People represented by Feoh are likely to be generous, sensual, and practical, but might also be judgmental, status-obsessed, and sometimes slow witted.

Feoh reversed or combined with particularly negative runes can signify a long period of hardship without obvious reward. The rune of wealth and status is also the rune of slavery.

Conversely, it can also represent indolence. So the nature of the other runes will need to help you decide which.

Feoh reversed can also represent loss of wealth both physical and emotional.

For magic, Feoh is a strange rune, and while it's primary use is for the gain of sustenance or wealth, it is also common in spells regarding the initiation or cementing of love.

Again, people do still marry for security (and wealth), and love is still frequently a power struggle and a slog.

Another oddity worthy of note is that I have seen it used at the beginning of ward spells and curses alike, which on the surface connect even less easily with the surface values of Feoh.

This aspect of Feoh may relate back to Audhumla, the primal cow. Using Audhumla's primal image, this first rune of the Futhark at the start of a spell may summon that great ancient power to consolidate any purpose, although it may just use the annotations of work to simply mean: "Make it happen…"

This use seems apparent in folk-lore where chants like "Fee Fie Fo Fum, I smell the blood of an English man…" in *Jack and the beanstalk,* and "Fee Fo, whoever grins gets a pinch a punch and a smack" in the poem *What You Got There?* (from Amabel Williams's *Fairies and Enchanters*).

I am wary of this particular use of Feoh, and advise the same. Feoh represents provision and thus power, but neither of these come without a price.

# Ur

ᚢ

*The Auroch is proud and has great horns*
*it is a very savage beast and fights with its horns;*
*a great ranger of the moors, it is a creature of mettle.*

Keywords: strength, tests, status, achievement, respect

Similarly to the first rune, Feoh, the second rune, Ur, represents oxen, although in a very different form.

Ur represents the wild side of oxen, in the form of the auroch.

The auroch was Northern Europe's answer to the buffalo until their extinction about a thousand years ago. They were big, they were wild, and they were an important food source for our hunter-gatherer ancestors. To hunt an auroch was a dangerous and difficult task, and this is why the hunting of these beasts was used as a symbol for the passage of young males into manhood. This dangerous test, as well as the formidable nature of the auroch — have you ever even been stuck in a field with a modern bull? It's scary — explains the meaning of Ur.

Ur is the rune of all things macho — that is to say, power, strength, status and ambition.

We are all confronted with tests, every day, which push us to the limits, and these challenges hopefully lead to a growth or promotion to some higher level of status or authority.

Where Ur appears in a reading, the time, or ability, to show off and impress others is heralded, whether it be in the form of an interview, a dangerous task or various types of male rutty sporting competitions, such as wrestling.

Ur's connotations of strength are a good omen to the unwell, or those about to face great physical hardship. You will be as 'strong as an ox'.

Ur is a great rune to invoke the strength and vitality of the auroch. Particularly great for the male body and mind, and combined with positive sex runes (such as Peorth, Birca, and Ing) or in reference to sex or love questions, Ur can assure the subject that physical attractiveness and prowess are not a problem.

Ur is an extremely gender-orientated rune and when used to identify someone, will nearly always refer to a man— although it could refer to the most dominant or butch person in question. People represented by this rune are usually brave, strong, and ambitious, but also can be arrogant, insensitive, and domineering.

Ur reversed can warn of a challenge that the questioner should not accept, or one which the questioner is doomed to fail — but it can also represent missed opportunities, or situations where the questioner would be a fool not to rise to the challenge. The surrounding runes should clarify this.

As a tool in magic, Ur is used to summon strength and courage, and to ready the user for challenges. It also promotes physical strength. I would avoid Ur in situations where sensitivity and tact are the dominant perquisites, as it represents raw strength and confidence in their elemental forms. These forces are not known for their subtlety. Manhood in all of it's embarrassingly clichéd archetypal forms, including the actual penis itself, are aided by Ur in magic. Be aware that other than the literal phallus, many of these attributes are sought and found in women, so Ur is not for 'men only' issues, but think butch and celebrate it here.

# Thorn

*The thorn is exceedingly sharp*
*an evil thing for any knight to touch*
*uncommonly severe on all who sit among them.*

Keywords: obstacles, strife, devil, Thor, protection

The rune Thorn is a complex rune, with a intricate pattern of symbolism, as opposed to one set image which the questioner can focus upon.

Thorn represents not only the sharp, sore to touch, protrusion on a plant that is the thorn itself, but Thor and the Jotuns as well, who are respectively the god of protection, and the equivalents of Christian demons. This might seem a very contradictory idea, but in legend Thor was the son of a Jotun, and his stormy but forthright attitudes to life were similar to those of his forebears. In this way, Thor, the Giants, and the very idea of the thorn itself were all seen as inter-connected and are expressed together with this one rune.

Thorn's Jotun nature means that it frequently represents obstacles and situations where one gets 'stuck' in a difficult, unsatisfactory or painful situation.

Where the questioner is looking for progress in any direction, be it career, love, travel, or the law, Thorn represents obstacles and periods of time where great caution and patience are required. When Thorn appears in a reading, you are likely to have to think hard before any action is undertaken, and it may be a bad idea altogether.

The Giants of the northern peoples were akin to the demons of Christianity. These Jotuns appear in legend as the sworn enemies of man and god alike. Thus, Thorn can represent adversaries, and maybe the questioner already knows that someone stands in their way.

However, due to Thor's role as protector, Thorn also represents protection from evil; if you are in a situation where you fear a great loss, Thorn's inhibiting powers can hold back any dangers. Indeed, magically, the rune Thorn is frequently used alone as a protection spell – however, it is a dangerous rune to cast complex spells with, as it could summon demons, as well as keep them away.

The way I like to explain this rune to people is to have them imagine they are stuck in a thick bush of thorns. This sounds like a terrible fate, but then I ask them to imagine that outside of these thorns is a bunch of really scary blokes with daggers. Suddenly, your thorn bush is a cherished home and, let's face it, Thor's strength is just what you need when defending yourself. Thor is the god of protection.

In situations where relationships are the concern, Thorn's pain and devilish nature may represent itself as arguments, upsets and a situation of deadlock.

Likewise with regards to issues of health, Thorn does not bring tidings of rapid progress to great comfort, but doesn't bode death either.

People represented by Thorn are wont to be blunt, stubborn, and cantankerous, but can they can equally be loyal, strong, and full of conviction.

Thorn reversed is never cheery, usually hinting at a situation where the questioner is likely to walk into a trap (often of their own making), create enemies, and make things worse by their own thoughtless actions. More tact is desperately needed in all areas where Thorn appears reversed.

Thorn is a popular talisman, and strangely safe for all of its associations.

A rune like Thorn with its array of negative traits may strike the reader as rare and unwise in magic, but it features regularly. Thorn is a powerful ward against almost anything and, by its association with the god Thor, even promotes good luck. Care has to be taken when combining it with other runes, as pain and antagonism are risks, but alone the rune Thorn is surprisingly auspicious, particularly with regards to protection.

Having said this, I would also be unlikely to choose it as a subject for meditation on its own, unless I was seeking the counsel of Thor.

Thorn would also not usually be on my list for health related spells. It is a great defender, but a poor releaser. Its connotations of pain would also trouble me.

## Ansur

ᚠ

*The mouth is the source of all language,*
*A pillar of wisdom and a comfort to wise men,*
*A blessing and a joy to every knight.*

Keywords: the mouth, wisdom, the father figure, talking, hearing, communicating.

Before understanding the rune Ansur, it is necessary to ask yourself why Odin, the King of the gods, is represented by the rune portraying the mouth.

It is no coincidence that, for most people, the word 'Viking' conjures an image of someone shouting invocations to the gods, even if it is a fat lady with a horned helmet banging out a Wagner aria. Neither is it a mistake that when Odin wishes to bless his most favoured son, Balder, he does it with runes carved on the boy's teeth for wise words.

The ancient Europeans believed, as I do, that words and sentences are the best gift that humanity has, as they transfer thoughts from one being to another. Using words, we can share our ideas and express our concerns or opinions. This ability enables us to do all of the amazingly wonderful, horrific, beautiful and ugly things that make us unique in the animal kingdom.

Ansur frequently represents this sharing of wisdom.

Sometimes it merely shows the wisdom of the reader, or their proposed action. However, often Ansur represents good advice that the questioner would be wise to heed, or answers that are already clear. Honesty is also to be trusted and respected.

Of course, the importance given to the spoken word by the ancients was also manifested in a profound dislike for unwise babble. Ansur invites the questioner to talk sincerely, and listen to the sincere.

Ansur is a good rune to use as an aid for challenging mental tasks, and situations where cunning is needed, as well as being a strong tool for 'calling' or invoking spirits or forces. The Norse people considered the voice a most powerful magical tool, using it to communicate to the spirits in the same way that we communicate with each other on the physical plane.

The father or teacher is sometimes represented by Ansur, as Ansur is the rune representing Odin, or the 'All-father', to use his other title. Maybe Ansur could represent the need to contact the questioner's father, or merely take the father into account, when considering one's next action, and if not, maybe there is an authority figure who can or should be considered.

People represented by Ansur are often elderly, or wise beyond their age.

They can be eloquent and talkative, though not prone to idle chatting.

Ansur reversed represents the lack of wisdom, or poor communication. It can represent lies, or information with-held, although usually these are the result of folly as opposed to ill intent. There are other runes that represent malevolent deceit more clearly.

Foolish prattle and slander are also possible, however.

Conversely, it can symbolise a silence where talk is needed, or that the questioner is not heeding the good advice of others.

Ansur reversed can also represent that more wisdom is required, generally. That some key issue is poorly understood, or missed entirely.

The accompanying runes or the subject at hand should help specify which of these.

As a talisman or part of a spell, Ansur invokes wisdom and the ability to communicate. That makes it a good choice for mentally stressful events like tests and interviews, as well as heated debates. The rune's focus is on tapping the wisdom around you and in the past, making it a good meditative rune for the inquisitive mind.

If you need to lie or withhold knowledge, Ansur is possibly a rune to avoid as it is a rune of truths, despite it being the rune of verbal mastery. Similarly, it could prove inconvenient if you turn out to be in error.

# Rad

ᚱ

*Riding seems easy to every warrior while he is indoors*
*and very courageous to him who traverses the high-roads*
*on the back of a stout horse.*

Keywords: riding, travel, holiday, visit, motion, cyclic motion, change

Rad is frequently linked by scholars to the 'Sun wheel', which is a metaphor for what the ancients perceived as the sun's daily passage around the world - thus it represents travelling, or the actual process of travelling.

When Rad appears, movement or the desire for movement are likely — and frequently a journey is imminent. Of course, there are many different kinds of journeying, and Rad can encompass many of them. Your journey could be a trip to the beach, visiting a friend or relative, or it may symbolise your embarking on a voyage. The accompanying Runes will determine the kind of change or travel.

However, the journeys or changes represented by Rad needn't be permanent, for Rad usually refers to errands and pleasure trips, with

the more earth-shattering runes Eh, and Lagu more likely representing voyages of no return. The journey of Rad, like the journey of the sun through the sky, is a cyclical route leading eventually back to almost exactly where it started. Where the travel is not a visit or holiday, Rad will more than likely represent a journey with no important destination.

In matters of the heart, Rad shows enjoyable times, romance and excitement, but without runes of a more permanent nature, Rad does not promise a lasting relationship.

People represented by Rad are travellers, if not literally, then in spirit. Fickleness, curiosity and a love of adventure will be manifest, along with alertness, a dislike of responsibility, and of course, itchy feet.

Rad is used to aid and protect travellers of body and mind, as well as to initiate travel.

Rad reversed foretells inconveniences and setbacks. Maybe a desired journey or change will be cancelled, or the questioner will have to leave their desired objectives and perform an annoying errand for other purposes. It can also represent pleasure trips that go sour and trouble whilst travelling.

In magic Rad is used to invoke or aid either travel or change. Rad gets things going, or hastens them back as required.

# Kaon

<

*The torch is known to every living man by its pale, bright flame;*
*It always burns where princes sit within.*

Keywords: discovery, enlightenment, understanding, visualisation, guidance

85

Spells: 'k' as in "cunning" or "keen"

The Rune Kaon represents the torch, and thus symbolises the coming of light and understanding into darkness and confusion. The torch is lit — and you can now see.

Where Kaon features, discoveries are made and secrets are disclosed.

If the questioner is confused or worried about resolving any mystery, then Kaon foretells that the solution is either on its way or is already within that person, and may be just waiting for the moment of truth. Kaon represents the torch — as such it can guide our way, as well as showing us answers to problems.

Kaon can also bring brilliant ideas and solutions to any walk of life, usually without help, unless otherwise indicated. The knowledge in question is either literally revealed, as if the lights were turned on — or else it is intuitively discovered already in your mind and is instantly obvious.

Unless this rune is combined with particularly unpleasant runes, or in regard to obviously dark secrets, the discovery made is likely to be of a positive nature. However, if the questioner were wishing to keep a secret, then Kaon would be a symbol that the discovery of their grand secret was imminent.

On the bright side, Kaon might be a sign that the truth was the best policy, anyway.

Kaon would represent an honest, intelligent person, attractive and striking in appearance.

Kaon reversed always refers to a lack of knowledge, or an important unknown factor. It can warn of nasty shocks and unpleasant discoveries or highlight the fact that the person in question is 'in the dark' with regards to the issue in hand.

Where nasty discoveries are hinted at, their discovery will be at least half of their remedy, as genuinely nasty surprises that could prove insoluble are usually signalled by the rune Peorth.

Sometimes, a lack of inspiration and ideas is hinted at with Kaon. Where enlightenment is sought, Kaon reversed would probably point towards continued ignorance.

In magic Kaon can be used to invite clarity to a situation, giving its user the ability to see their way through problems and find solutions. This makes it a strong rune for spiritual pursuits. Obviously, the one instance when you should truly avoid using Kaon for magic is when you are hiding something or lying. In this way Kaon is the "Out" rune, albeit with a smile. Kaon is a great rune to start with for meditation, along with a good fire.

Kaon is the rune that asks for enlightenment.

# Gyfu

X

*Generosity brings credit and honour, which support one's dignity;*
*it furnishes help and subsistence*
*to all broken men who are devoid of ought else.*

Keywords: Gift, meet, exchange, contact, communication, relationship, sacrifice

Spells: 'g' as in 'gift' or 'gate'

Gyfu is one of the few runes that do not obviously represent anything physical. In fact, Gyfu literally represents an exchange of sorts, whether it be a gift or a meeting. This rune thus represents interaction between people and their relationships with each other, as well as people's relationships with the spirit world.

All people and animals rely on their ability to interact with each other to choose sexual partners, business colleagues and social groups. Gyfu represents this ability that we all need and which we all have — to some extent. Gyfu makes us aware that our relationships with other people mould our life as much as anything else.

Gyfu often represents meetings with people who are either already important in life, or people that are going to be. Sometimes Gyfu can represent gifts, either received or given, to establish contact.

Gyfu is an easily swayed rune, and while it cannot be reversed, the mood of Gyfu is largely decided by the runes beside it. Positive runes beside Gyfu represent people helping each other, exchanging gifts and communicating.

Combined with other love runes, Gyfu can speak of the most perfect love, a union of souls and minds.

Combined with negative or aggressive runes, Gyfu foretells arguments, selfishness and the neglect of each other's needs and feelings.

Gyfu can represent people who are generous, understanding, and affectionate, but it can also represent people who mould their opinions to suit their environment. This trait could be read as insincerity.

For magic, Gyfu is one of the runes to use if you wish to get closer to someone. Not necessarily love, but including love. It represents interaction in a good way, and the exchange of gifts.

This frequent actor in love spells still appears at the end of letters to loved ones worldwide, as kisses.

Gyfu is also an important rune for magic in general, representing, along with Ing, your contact and exchanges with the spiritual world. In this way, Gyfu often appears in spells that do not seem otherwise wholly relevant.

The importance of Gyfu in magic reminds us that nothing comes for free. If you already know people who are involved in magic of any form, they will probably have told you that their 'gifts' came with demands.

# Wunna

*Bliss he enjoys who knows not suffering, sorrow nor anxiety, and has prosperity and happiness and a good enough house.*

Keywords: Joy, Friend, Contentment, Fun

Spells: 'w' as in 'wonderful' or 'growing'

The happiness that Wunna represents is both sincere and pure.

Because the pleasure or happiness that Wunna indicates is based on neither greed nor pride, it is not only the rarest, but also the most intense pleasure — and because it is not fed by any desire or necessity, it is sustainable.

This happiness comes to us all in various ways, possibly through the meeting of close friends, or maybe even a hobby.

It could be a job that you enjoy doing or people who make you smile. Wunna is one of the few runes that simply can never be read in a negative way, unless the questioner seriously wants to be miserable forever.

Wunna therefore is pure, untainted happiness, sometimes even holy, mystical, or pious joy.

People represented by Wunna are a pleasure to be with. They could be a close friend or someone good to have fun and relax with.

Wunna reversed represents a lack of the above. Dissatisfaction or active displeasure in either what you are doing or who you are doing it with.

As a straight forward talisman Wunna encourages friendship and happiness. This importantly includes happiness and harmony in the work place, meaning harmony with peers and pleasure in the tasks at hand.

Worn as a charm, Wunna encourages friendliness, a sense of fun, and the ability to enjoy the simple things in life.

# Hagal's eight

## Hagal

ᚺ

*Hail is the whitest of grain;*
*it is whirled from the vault of heaven*
*and is tossed about by gusts of wind*
*and then it melts into water*

Keywords: Hail, weather, health, unpredictable, rapid, unplanned,
Spells: 'h' as in 'hail'

Even today, and in the Western world, the weather still plays a massive role in how pleasant our lives can be. Farmers can still have their crops ruined by hail, and days can be made a joy or a misery depending on what the sky hurls at us. Hagal represents this very phenomenon.

Where Hagal appears anything could happen or, more accurately, the gods are to decide the next link in the chain of events.

An irreversible rune, it is neither negative nor positive, and its sway between the two must be gleaned either from nearby runes, or relevance to the subject in hand.

Combined with negative runes, Hagal usually represents the sort of surprises that we'd all rather do without, but reminds us that these are all part of the wonder of life. Hagal frequently represents the kind of disaster that can happen in an instant, as hail might appear to come from nowhere and devastate a field of corn in a single night. Life can be ambling along quite pleasantly, when all of a sudden something appears out of the blue and sends everything into chaos. This sort of occurrence is inconvenient and unpleasant, but it must be accepted as the will of the gods.

In the same way, however, miracles can also happen and turn what seems to be a disastrous situation into a happy one — and this can happen just as easily.

93

If there is a marked desire for haste in your life, Hagal is your friend. Hagal, although destructive, has great cleansing powers and often brings about an end that is long overdue. Whether it's a long awaited conclusion or the end to a long period of suffering, Hagal is often that needed promise of change.

Illnesses and long-standing troubles are frequently waved goodbye by Hagal, as it is not only a symbol of things which come and go in a flash, but it is also a symbol of purity and nature, foretelling good health.

People represented by Hagal are likely to be violently changeable in mood and lifestyle, although they will be likely also to live by a very high moral code.

I personally use this rune frequently to deal with issues of physical, mental, and spiritual disease, as it has great cleansing power. This trait of Hagal is still traceable in modern British society, where some people still say: "Hail the Queen" (although not very often, where I live). This literally means "Good health to the Queen". Hagal is a good purifier for before and after any magical exercises.

# Niet

## †

*Trouble is oppressive to the heart;*
*yet often it proves a source of help and salvation*
*to the children of men, to everyone who heeds it betimes.*

Keywords: trouble, need, restriction, care, patience, caution, deftness
Spells: 'n' as in 'not' or 'knot'

Although there are varying opinions as to what Niet actually represents, many rune practitioners suggest that Niet is the need-fire, which is a fire that has been lit by the process of rubbing two sticks together, using a bow. Whilst other symbolism, including 'the knot'

94

and the abstract concept of 'need', also have relevance, this analogy with the need-fire fits just too well for me not to use it.

Lighting a 'need fire', despite what survival enthusiasts may say, is an absolute pain. It's fiddly, and with anything but ideal conditions, it's arduous. From what we can tell, it was as loathed a task in the 1st 1000 years BCE as it would be now. Indeed, the Celts disliked it so much that they all shared the task, and did it only once a year, at Yule, and would simply never let their fires go out until the following year.

Frequently, we find ourselves having to face the fact that the situation in front of us will not be resolved overnight. Niet represents troublesome objectives, and times where great care and patience is needed to achieve the desired results. These will be problems that cannot be easily overcome, and tasks that the questioner will have to work through patiently and carefully.

In a reading, Niet usually means that the questioner will also have to tread prudently if they do not wish to make things worse. This rune is representative of the fact that we sometimes have to learn through hardship and our past mistakes.

In matters of poor health, Niet is no great comfort, as it symbolises uphill struggles — sometimes very long ones — although it is commonly used magically to provide strength to people suffering from potentially fatal conditions.

On the bright side, Niet has connotations of intelligence as well as endurance, and can frequently be seen as a call for the use of the brain and thought — as opposed to the use of brawn and gut instinct. So, the one circumstance where Niet can be seen as a positive influence on a reading is where the intellect is being tested. In this context, Niet assures that questioner that their mind is up to it, as long as the necessary concentration is given.

An ideal study rune, Niet's presence in a reading about educational issues works as an assurance of ability, although contained within is a warning that there is still a need for hard work.

Niet also sometimes represents sacrifices that need to be made - sometimes for your goal, and sometimes for others. The thing to remember is that each time these trials and sacrifices need to be made, the knowledge you have is greater and that the reward will be worth it.

Usually, melancholy and pessimistic, yet wise and enduring people are represented by this rune.

Niet reversed does not make for cheerful reading and represents nasty mistakes, the repercussions of which may last a long time. The questioner is likely to attempt too much and crack under the strain, or may just make things considerably worse by trying what seems to be the easy way.

Foolishness and recklessness are the stuff of Niet reversed. There may be obvious warnings that are likely to go unheeded.

Niet is a risky rune in magic. If you know that a long slog is ahead, and only if you know that, Niet may help provide the patience and endurance needed to see it through. Sufferers of severe and long-term illness can benefit from Niet, but beware. While Niet can keep people alive, it can actually block their recovery.

Niet is another wisdom rune, but there are nearly always better alternatives.

It is also the rune that governs difficult tasks, like starting a fire by rubbing sticks, so it could prove handy there.

## Iss

|

*Ice is very cold and immeasurably slippery;*
*it glistens as clear as glass and most like to gems;*
*it is a floor wrought by the frost, fair to look upon.*

Keywords: stasis, halt, standstill, reflection, perception, observer

Spells: 'i' as in 'ice' or *'i' as in* 'idle'

Ice is cold, harsh, slippery and treacherous, but it is also transparent. Everything caught in it is forced into a state of complete stillness. Iss, therefore, is symbolic... both of stasis and of vision.

Iss can represent a period of peace and a time to reflect, but where change or motion is desired, Iss is, of course, the enemy.

This rune often represents the fact that a situation is not progressing, and has come to a total halt. In this way, Iss can represent a period of peace and a time to reflect, although more often than not this means forced inaction and a situation of complete powerlessness.

There are in fact times in life where there is nothing left to do but sit and reflect. Sometimes we all need to step out of our problems and watch for a while. Perhaps there is something that the questioner needs to observe before they can carry on.

In relationships, Iss is not auspicious, as it can signal coldness or a lack of feeling. The relationship may be stale, or may be at the point of deadlock where no one will budge an inch.

Iss is also of no comfort to the ill, as it can indicate that their ailments are likely to linger. An awaited recovery is going to be held back, for the questioner must wait in Iss' cold shroud.

However, like Thorn, Iss is a good rune for defence, because ice preserves things. If you are worried about losing something, it is held fast.

Iss is also the rune of the eyes and sight, and sometimes that of inner sight. If answers are being sought after, Iss is a positive sign. Iss is also a great rune for people who wish to find that which is lost, or it may similarly allow the questioner to see the unseen in its many forms. Ice is translucent, and the winter ice peels back the vegetation of the jumbled forest floor. Iss can frequently be a sign that a questioner just needs to stop and look to find what they seek.

Iss signifies the human traits of intelligence, observation skills and beauty — but these are paired with coldness, treachery and harshness.

For static objects Iss can serve as a protecting charm, by proverbially covering it in ice.

For people, it can provide calm and clarity of thought, but potentially at the cost of coldness and melancholy. I personally would think hard before wearing it around my neck. Iss is good for eye related health conditions, but for almost all other health issues it is worth avoiding. Generally, I would advise against using Iss on animals or people before you really feel that you know what you're doing.

As a meditation rune it represents clarity and purity, but again this comes with melancholy and coldness if you are not careful.

# Jera

ᛃ

*Summer is a joy to men, when God, the holy King of Heaven,*
*suffers the earth to bring forth shining fruits*
*for rich and poor alike.*

Keywords: reward, justice, fruition, law, divine law, result

Spells: 'j' as in 'judge', or 'y' as in 'year'

Jera literally translates as year and is also specifically related to the cyclical nature of the year.

Even those who live on the Equator live at the mercy of the seasons, and the nearer you get to either the North or South Pole, the more extreme these seasons are.

However, while the peoples of the North keenly felt the pangs of winter, they were not altogether at its mercy. These people were able to farm their fertile lands, and with their carefully grown and tended foods they could survive the barren winter. This brings us to the fundamental nature of the Rune Jera. Jera not only represents the year, but a significant mark in the year of the Northern Hemisphere. Jera represents the time of Harvest, where the fruits and farm crops are gathered for the winter.

Harvest would be a time of joy if the crops had done well; but people would starve in the winter if not.

It is a time when all of our efforts are repaid with the fruits of our labour, and in this way justice is represented by Jera. Jera is a positive sign usually, but as representative of justice, Jera metes out punishment with reward. If no effort is put into this life, nothing, or worse, is often received in return.

Often it represents the point where all actions have been taken, and we must simply await the result. Most of the time, however, Jera signifies the time when we are finally rewarded for our efforts and

trials. The questioner should know which of these is the case; long term stuff like Jera is usually easily recognised.

Physically irreversible, Jera is heavily influenced by other runes, as well as by its context. On it's own it is a modestly positive sign, but with negative runes it is easily soured.

Because of the emphasis Jera has on justice, it can sometimes represent legal actions and trials. This is particularly true when other runes are of an intellectual or judiciary feel.

If you are working hard for something that you expect no return on for a long time, or await the results of past effort, Jera may be a good rune for contemplation.

Similarly, Jera is an excellent charm for all things agricultural, as it represents the yearly cycle that crops depend on.

It is also associated with spells regarding justice, yet it would be foolish to wear it if you deserved anything but the best. Jera is the Karma rune.

As a symbol of cyclic activity, it can be used help to maintain processes of an on going or cyclic nature.

# Yr

ᛦ

*The yew is a tree with rough bark,*
*hard and fast in the earth, supported by its roots,*
*a guardian of flame and a joy upon an estate.*

Keywords: Strength, turmoil, night, tolerance, survival, defence
  Spells: 'y' as in 'you' or 'happy' and 'i' as in 'ink'
  Yr literally translates as 'yew tree'.

The yew tree is a moderately sized conifer known primarily for its tough wood, poisonous properties, and ability to live on for thousands of years.

From pre-history, yew has been used to make weapons and yet stands ironically as a symbol of eternal life. In ancient societies yew trees were often used to mark the graves of important people, a tradition that passed right into the Middle Ages, and yews are still a common sight in churchyards today. It is still considered by many to be bad luck to bring yew wood into the house without 'permission' from the tree.

Yr represents life and strength in the face of adversity. In readings, Yr frequently represents times of turmoil and fear, but at the same time it also offers the strength to survive them.

Yr cannot be said to be a positive rune, as it always refers to anxiety or even fear and hardship.

Frequently Yr appears as a representative of a crisis or disaster that seems to threaten the very existence of the questioner, or their sanity.

Yr, however, has one great upside... it is the rune of survival.

Ironically, Yr, the rune that most definitely spells out a period of turmoil, is also the rune that reassures the questioner that they will survive this time. Yr tells us that we will be all the better for any negative experience if we can just hold on.

So, while Yr spells out sorrow and fear for the near future, it comforts us with the knowledge that whatever is thrown our way, it won't be enough to defeat us.

You will come through strong — says Yr — and for this reason, Yr represents strong, courageous and patient people.

Yr, like Niet, can be used as a charm to see you through arduous times, this time particularly where peril is perceived. With Yr emphasis is on your courage and durability in difficult times. Again, I'd only use it in said difficult times, or it may actually bring them on.

It is the nearest we have to a night rune.

Many believe that the legendary tree of life, Yggdrasil, is a yew tree, although this isn't totally clear from what records we have.

Yr is the rune of endurance.

# Peorth

*Peorth is a source of recreation and amusement to the great,*
*where warriors sit blithely together in the banqueting-hall.*

Keywords: secrets, mysteries, pleasure, sex, the unknown, whispers

Spells: 'p' as in 'pepper' or 'suprise'

The literal meaning of Peorth has long been debated, and various ideas are around. These have included — the hearth, the apple, the dice cup, the vagina and the hall — all of which are frequent suggestions.

Strangely, though, the meaning of this rune is generally agreed upon. Peorth represents the revealing, unlocking or manifestation of the concealed.

With Peorth, information withheld from you is suddenly revealed, not by forceful acts of discovery, but when you are deemed ready.

In this way, Peorth can herald your initiation into grand secrets, or truths that not everyone can obtain.

Peorth is often the rune of mystery and delight, and the pleasure of the Peorth sort can be obtained in many ways. This pleasure could be obtained through the unlocking of secrets, through sex, by intoxicating substances (such as alcohol), by mystical experiences, by eating, or even by laughter, for instance.

However, many of these pleasures need to be treated with respect and caution. Misused, or over-indulged, these pleasures and surprises can become dangers. Peorth heralds pleasure and excitement. It also signals secrecy and intrigue, but frequently there is something sinister to be aware of as well, and maybe even to avoid.

Peorth frequently is merely the sign of an enjoyable experience, and can symbolise spiritual growth. But Peorth is unpredictable, and for that reason it is unsafe.

In Peorth, truths are explored and revealed, but there is no guarantee that they will be as pleasant as they are intriguing.

In readings, particularly in positions regarding the future, Peorth can signal that this secret must be met without the Runes. You are not meant to know.

Peorth reversed represents nasty surprises, and problems with no known answers. It can pinpoint disease, treachery and danger.

Peorth reversed advises extreme caution.

Peorth is the rune of the stranger. The stranger that you have not met, and the stranger that you thought you knew. Peorth should only be used with great caution in spells. It is the mystery rune, and can unlock mysteries good and bad. Peorth alone can both reveal and hide secrets if so desired but be careful when combining it, as you may inadvertently choose an unintended result. Peorth is volatile.

As the keeper of mysteries, Peorth actually does suit meditation, and a nice real fire is a great place to do this. It could be unpredictable though, so I would recommend getting to know this rune after a few of the easier and mellower runes.

Peorth as a charm can guard secrets.

Peorth is the sex, drugs and rock and roll rune. Were I to meet someone wearing this as a charm, I would come to the conclusion that their name began with "P", or that they were looking for a wild time.

# Eohll

ᛉ

*The Eohll-sedge is mostly to be found in a marsh;*
*it grows in the water and makes a ghastly wound,*
*covering with blood every warrior who touches it.*

Keywords: Spirit, protection, guidance, wisdom, instinct
Spells 'a' as in 'hay' or 'sail' (debated)

The exact meanings and pronunciation of Eohll are debated amongst mystics and scholars alike — a strange thing because Eohll is present in all Futhark variants. The Anglo-Saxon meaning is offered as the sedge — a grasslike plant with triangular stems that are found typically in wet ground, and widely distributed throughout temperate and cold regions — although this meaning is not the most widely regarded. Other possibilities include the axe, the arms outstretched, the deer and the vagina. Hopefully, this will explain why the passage above and the description below are not wildly similar.

Ironically, Eohll's spiritual meaning is rarely disputed or contradicted. Eohll represents protection and the spiritual.

Eohll is a good sign if one is anxious, for it is a protector. It can be the representative of a spirit mother, or angel, and signifies that you are safe and in good hands. Eohll also sometimes even represents your physical mother, and the help and advice that she can give.

Equally, Eohll represents inner truths. Frequently, if one is perplexed by some grand mystery, Eohll tells us that the answer will come from within.

When negative runes accompany Eohll, then the questioner may be discouraged by outside influences, but should probably stand strong to their convictions. The message is usually that their inner judgement will be right.

In readings about relationships, Eohll can represent honesty and closeness, or a person who will not let their guard down. How promising the other runes are will decide which of these is the case.

The people signified by Eohll are usually women who are independent, caring, and honest, but possibly a touch aloof.

When reversed, Eohll represents lies, and whereas the untruths of Ansur reversed are untrue through ignorance, the lies of Eohll are intentional and motivated. Eohll reversed frequently tells you that your guard needs to go up, and that you are trusting unworthy people.

Perhaps, Eohll offers -that the questioner cannot accept the truth and lies to themselves.

Eohll reversed signals a time where you must question yourself and not be too gullible. It is worthy of note that Eohll also (only rarely) represents aggression when reversed. A destructive power, or a will to destroy.

A set of events highlighted by Eohll reversed are not in the name of good or in anyone's favour, unless these individuals take pleasure from the pain of those around them.

109

You can imagine that for magic, Eohll is an obvious choice.

It is the most important protection rune.

In a strange paradox, the same rune is used to drive away dangers evoke and invite benevolent forces.

My personal understanding of this is that Eohll, in this magical sense, is the equivalent of presenting yourself and your intentions.

It is a bit like the advice: If you are being followed head somewhere public. Being seen is sometimes being safe.

Even more so than Ansur, Eohll is a bad choice for the liar, but it makes up for this by being an excellent choice for the foolish. Wearing or using Eohll in magic is a declaration of self. Consider it as the magical equivalent of getting up and waving your arms about.

Eohl could be said to be the rune of the soul or spirit.

Eohll has obvious connections with the physical gestures of opening your arms to greet someone, or shoo a beast, which is handy in meditation and magic. It is also represented more subtly by holding your hand up with three fingers outstretched and thumb and pinky folded in.

# Sig

ᛋ

*The sun is ever a joy in the hopes of seafarers*
*when they journey away over the fishes' bath,*
*until the courser of the deep bears them to land.*

Keywords: victory, success, triumph against all odds, winning, conquest

Spells: 's' as in 'sun', or 'z' as in 'zoo'

Sig is the rune of the sun, but not in its normal and nourishing guise. The sun ascribed to Sig is the sun that legendarily turns vampires and devils into dust. Many runic practitioners have noted that Sig resembles a thunder bolt, and it is with similar power that Sig is associated.

Along with Tyr, Sig was a popular rune for Viking warriors to have engraved on their swords. This is because monsters seem to just burn up in its glorious light.

Sig is nearly always a positive rune. It foretells the removal of setbacks, or even the vanquishing of one's enemies.

It is not a halfway rune, yet it does not always signify aggression and is equally emblematic of the end of a horrid time, or the completion of a difficult or annoying task.

Of course, if you have had a disagreement with someone, then Sig represents an out and out win for you, as opposed to a well thought-out agreement, or an understanding that has been reached. The message is that you'll win — and they'll lose.

Sig represents not just success, but a glory of some kind. If the victory is the completion of a task or trial, it will probably seem like a success despite the environmental factors, as opposed to with them. Sig in this way signals an achievement made against the odds.

Where long waits are a problem, Sig promises the desired energy to get things moving.

Sig is non-reversible and is generally a good rune, and can cheer up most readings. However, in my experience, when someone's attitudes are under examination, Sig could be a warning that they are being overly blunt or aggressive.

Sig would represent a powerful, confident, and even heroic person, but they may also be slightly domineering or aggressive.

In magic Sig is raw power - it brings victory by dispelling evil dramatically - but beware. If you are the one in the wrong, it can turn on you. I have to say that in magic, I actively avoid this rune. Like a weapon, most of the people who are drawn to it are best advised to avoid it.

It is a positive sign, and sometimes needed, but represents the kind of power best summarised by the Hindu god Shiva, who embodies, among other things, destruction, particularly the destruction of ignorance. Are you sure enough to invite Shiva to solve your problems with a pure and un-bendable justice that may or may not serve your favour? If so, feel free to use Sig.

# Tyr's eight

## Tyr

↑

*Tiw is a guiding star; well does it keep faith with princes;*
*it is ever on its course over the mists of night and never fails.*

Keywords: Conviction, Purpose, Courage, Justice

Spells: 't' as in 'time'

Tyr represents victory, but unlike Sig, it is usually a mental victory.

An inner victory and improvement of your own circumstances is suggested by Tyr, as opposed to the victory of ousting others.

Periods of indecision and feeling without purpose or direction are distressing to us all, and useful to none. Tyr symbolises the capability to choose the right direction and do the right thing.

Unless the surrounding runes are negative, Tyr will mean that you are on the right track, and that your conviction will pay off.

Sometimes Tyr represents a situation where you are standing up to what you believe in or know is right.

Tyr also sometimes represents legal affairs, and communicates to the questioner that those who stick to the truth will end up on top. The god Tyr was the protector of oaths, and Vikings would call him as their witness when swearing on their swords.

The message might be: without believing in what you do, nothing truly wonderful can be achieved.

Tyr represents older people. It also represents the virtues - bravery, wisdom and justice. People indicated by Tyr may even be involved with justice or legal matters.

When reversed, Tyr represents poor decisions.

The questioner may be choosing the wrong path, or may simply not have committed to anything in particular, thus straying aimlessly — a dangerous pursuit.

Such a person may also be party to something immoral and simply adhering to it, either because it's easier for them or they don't have the guts to come out and say it.

Tyr reversed could represent the need to bite the bullet and take the right path. It could represent being lost altogether, but usually it denotes the lack of faith as the problem.

A magical practice that seeks a victory of sorts may be better served by Tyr than Sig. Tyr provides not only the strength and resolution to see a task through, but the wisdom to direct a situation towards the greater good.

Difficult decisions are best faced with Tyr or Ansur. Like Sig, Tyr is a poor servant for the morally objectionable unless they are swayable, which in this case can serve to set them right.

## Birca

ᛒ

*The poplar bears no fruit; yet without seed it brings forth suckers,*
*for it is generated from its leaves.*
*Splendid are its branches and gloriously adorned*
*It's lofty crown, which reaches to the skies.*

Keywords: beginnings, new, planning, springtime, hatching, births
Spells: 'b' as in 'baby' or 'cub'
Birca represents the mother and fertility. Birth has many forms, and all of them beautiful. Whether they are the abstract births of ideas or artwork or the real births of children and life — all are wonderful.

The conception of all of these is symbolized by Birca, the mother.

 115

This rune often heralds new ideas and plans, as well as actual pregnancy and birth. This rune, unless accompanied by negative runes, tells us that our new plans and conceptions are going to be a success.

If the surrounding runes are negative, try and see if they can be read as pitfalls, or possible obstacles that you will need to resolve these before progressing.

Birca is also a reminder to us of the profound role that our mothers play in our creation; it reminds us to respect them as our creators.

Birca represents mothers, motherhood, and infants. In this way, Birca can reflect caring roles. This new thing, this plan, this child will need love.

Birca reversed represents the plans, projects and things not to be. Maybe these projects or plans are not being nurtured properly — or maybe they just don't work. This could signal the sadness of seeing a dream ending, or in fact never in fact starting. Birca reversed can point to illness or, very rarely, death. Usually, though, it is just the collapse of something you wanted.

As a fertility rune, Birca is an obvious choice for aiding childbirth and the rearing of children. It is also by this virtue a strong rune for the blessing of new plans, as well as creativity in general.

It's fertility connections also make it a useful rune for allure and romance, but not without risk of pregnancy, so be careful. In the field of romance it represents the specific trait of allure.

# Eh

ᛗ

*The horse is a joy to princes in the presence of warriors.*
*A steed in the pride of its hoofs,*
*when rich men on horseback bandy words about it;*
*and it is ever a source of comfort to the restless.*

Keywords: travel, change, progress, partner, party

117

Spells: 'e' as in 'better' or 'let'

If you happen to travel by horse, then Eh may represent that horse — for most of us however, Eh comes as a sign that we are about to move on.

Travel or change is often on the cards, and this is usually of a permanent nature.

Life can be described as a one way trip.

Life, or an aspect of it, will take suddenly change direction, and this change will be for the better.

The horse also represents those around you that will help you on your way.

Eh can often represent loyal friends, or people who share your aims, and will help you reach your goals.

When surrounded by restrictive or static runes, Eh can merely foretell the desire to move on, and may point to a time of feeling unsettled or frustrated. It is hard to read Eh entirely negatively.

Those represented by Eh are your friends and associates — the people around you who are there to help.

Sometimes Eh is there to tell you that you should value your friends or ask them for help. In this way, Eh can be the traveller's friend more than it is their path.

Eh reversed means travelling barefoot. You might be about to realise that your friend is not going your way, or that you have no horse. People around may abandon or even hinder you — possibly people you had hitherto thought you could depend upon.

This is not betrayal, however. Eh reversed reminds us that people who are poorly aligned to our needs are not necessarily malevolent. They are probably just heading their own way.

Eh reversed may also suggest that it is not a good time to travel. As the rune of the friend and helper of man, Eh is a great charm for those seeking friendship and support on their way. Perhaps surprisingly, it features in love spells quite frequently. It is a comfort to think that rune mages reliably count friendship and support as so tantamount. Obviously Eh is a blessing to the traveller - possibly the best.

# Mann

ᛗ

*The joyous man is dear to his kinsmen;*
*yet every man is doomed to fail his fellow,*
*since the Lord by his decree will commit the vile carrion to the earth.*

Keywords: people, gatherings, institutions, rules, public

Spells: 'm' as in 'man' or 'meter'

Mann is a symbol of mankind; civilization and institutions are often denoted by this rune. These can be courts, places of study, hospitals or churches.

You may well find yourself in one of these institutions, for one of many reasons. People often go to places of worship or learning for education – and guidance — or maybe you are involved in the running of an institution. Basically, Mann represents gatherings of people for any purpose.

If justice runes are present, a legal action may be imminent.

If the surrounding runes are love runes, marriage may be denoted - marriage, in any form, is the public declaration of love or devotion.

The need to communicate in general is emphasized by Mann, as is the need to fit into society as a whole.

Mann is an ancient word that depicts the whole of human society, and it should not be seen as gender specific.

Those represented by Mann are usually people who live or work in the public eye — for example, doctors, teachers, actors, preachers, managers and others.

Mann reversed represents people, organisations or systems that you will have to struggle with. Poor communication and relationships are pointed to. Struggles with rules and society, including the law, can be symbolised; but usually Mann reversed points to something as simple as friction, or obstacles created by your peers.

Mann reversed can also represent disconnectedness and loneliness.

In magic and meditation, Mann is particularly useful to those who are either seeking, or already reckoning with, attention of the general public or large institutions. This includes business, law, education, public declarations and even the pursuit of fame. Any rune spell involving lengthy negotiation or public relations would be likely to involve Mann.

Mann is a good charm for marriage, as it represents good communication, as well as the declaration involved. Marriage is the public declaration and contract of love.

# Lagu

ᚱ

*The ocean seems interminable to men,*
*if they venture on the rolling bark*
*and the waves of the sea terrify them*
*and the courser of the deep heed not its bridle.*

Keywords: life, flowing, emotions, receptivity

Spells: 'l' as in 'lady' or 'lake'

Lagu is the rune of deep water, and nature; it is the great sea and the water of life.

It symbolises a force both treacherous and life giving — the emotions are symbolised by Lagu, as is the subconscious.

Many of these things have more control over us than we have over them, and Lagu is often a sign that we may feel as if we are merely drifting through life.

This lack of control can be both relaxing and terrifying — due to this, creative processes such as music and art are often represented by Lagu. Ideas being created intuitively are also represented.

Like Rad and Eh, Lagu can be a portent of travel – however, this can be metaphorical. Unlike Rad and Eh, Lagu's journey is likely to involve the need to let go, and trust fate to an extent. Often this means that these travels are of a grander nature. Whether they are internal journeys or literally hopping on a train, they are likely to be life changing.

The nature of the runes surrounding it will very much govern the mood of Lagu — Negative runes represent the loss of control, and a descent in to chaos, while positive runes signify the riding of this strange tide and having an exciting, fulfilling adventure.

Lagu is a love rune, and surrounded by positive emotional runes, it can represent the romantic in life.

People connected to Lagu are usually emotional, artistic and rely heavily on intuition. Lagu is a female sign, and often denotes women.

Lagu reversed represents loss and lack of control. Life can drag you the wrong way. You may need to be particularly decisive to not be dragged where you do not want to go. Conversely, you may be forced to accept it.

Lagu also represents emotional turmoil and storms swelling in your heart. In readings regarding relationships, expect a rough ride.

Used in magic, Lagu allows you to get in touch with the rolling and unpredictable forces of life both external and internal. Where Eohll could be seen as the soul, Lagu is the ether that it navigates as well as the blood that drives it.

I would choose a lake or the sea as a place to contemplate Lagu.

Lagu can help you take control of these creative, emotional or unpredictable forces - but not completely. The forces that Lagu governs can be ridden, and even steered at times, but never controlled outright.

Lagu can be used to restore creative and spiritual flows, as well as to get in touch with emotions, but on the understanding that easy rides are not guaranteed.

Lagu can also be good for health matters, particularly those regarding circulation or plumbing.

Lagu is a life rune, so it can be called upon where life and death are in question - but remember that this is the chaotic life rune.

A possibly silly, but revealing, warning is that Lagu is a poor guardian of inanimate objects that you value, or things that you want to keep.

Lagu is liberating.

# Ing

*Ing was first seen by men among the East-Danes,*
*till, followed by his chariot,*
*he departed eastwards over the waves.*
*So the Heardingas named the hero.*

Keywords: creativity, beginning, end, finished, starting, male

Spells: 'ng' as in 'running' or 'song'

Ing is the rune of running water and fertility. It represents fertility, either in a creative sense, where ideas flow, or in a natural and biological sense.

Particularly when combined with Birca or another female rune, Ing can symbolise the act of sex, and also the conception of a child.

Ing often represents the completion of one project and the commencement of a newer and better one, thus frequently representing progress.

Ing is a rune that can lighten up any reading, as it stands for satisfactory conclusions and wonderful new beginnings. Ing indicates that solutions to problems might literally to drop out of the sky.

Artwork and music are often represented by Ing, as are dreams and mystical experiences.

People represented by Ing are creative, intuitive and positive. Ing is a masculine sign and usually portrays a young man, but not always.

Ing cannot be reversed and cannot be read negatively unless it is surrounded by very dark runes. Maybe you didn't want a baby — and this is where Ing's hints at fertility might displease you.

Ing is a good rune for spells regarding finishing up old projects or starting new ones, as well as promoting novel ideas. Like Lagu, it

is one of the arty runes, but this time with stability. Ing represents the birth of ideas.

Ing also frequently appears in love spells, representing sex in a good way.

Like Feoh and Gyfu, Ing is often used as an instigator or empowering element for otherwise unrelated spells - if you really feel the need for this, Ing is much safer.

It often features at the beginning and end of otherwise unrelated spells, as a kind of, 'this really is a magical thing' marker.

Ing is also hard to turn dark, unlike Gyfu which is wholly positive in its own right but easily swayed.

The only cautionary message I have about Ing regards its association with fertility. If you're not feeling expert and don't want babies, it might be a good idea to hold back on Ing.

Head to the river or the sea if you wish to parlay with Ing.

# Othel

*An estate is very dear to every man,*
*if he can enjoy there in his house*
*whatever is right and proper in constant prosperity.*

Keywords: Home, Homeland, house, family, stable, settled
Spells: 'o' as in 'odd' or 'ode'

Othel represents your immoveable wealth. Certain things that you own are fixed where they are, such as your home and your homeland.

These things provide stability and a foundation — and thus Othel represents that security.

When making plans, Othel is a signifier of your 'foundations', and denotes whether your plans or projects are built on solid grounds.

However, as immoveable, such grounds can act as a hindrance if you feel the need to move on or progress in another way.

Othel frequently represents things that will either have to be left behind if you move on — or things that will actually prevent your travels.

Thus, in a reading where travel or change runes are prolific, Othel can be a negative rune, representing the things that hold you back. Sometimes Othel can also be seen as advice that moving on or changing will involve great sacrifices that outweigh the benefits of the transition.

Othel is sometimes present in a reading as a signal that you are far from home, or that a time to re-visit your roots is long overdue.

Othel as a home rune can represent parents, relatives and even ancestors. Please note that you have birthplace 'ancestors' as well as genetic ones, and Othel frequently represents the former.

Sometimes, when what seems to be a new problem faces us, going back to our roots may show things in a more familiar light.

Othel represents the traditional, and people with a strong sense of tradition. Whether this adherence to the past should be seen as good or bad depends on the situation.

Othel often represents family members and old friends.

Othel is a rune that can be used to provide stability. It calls on the ground beneath you, and your background, to provide this. Its static nature makes is a poor choice for dynamic experiences like the moving on or dispelling of the undesired, but where stability is required it is a strong rune. It also has strong connection with the past and could be a wise rune to meditate upon with regards to the past - particularly with regards to your own.

As it represents stability, Othel is a good rune for house blessings and the homestead in its own right as a place of belonging, and refuge, from the outer world.

# Dag

*Day, the glorious light of the Creator, is sent by the Lord;*
*it is beloved of men, a source of hope and happiness to rich and poor,*
*and of service to all.*

Keywords: dawn, understanding, conclusion, peace
Spells: 'd' as in 'day' and 'paddle'
Dag is the most positive of all of the runes — it represents the dawn.

Your problems or fears will now seem resolved, or insignificant. All that remains is the glory of a new day and a new beginning.

Dag can never be read negatively as it represents a period of hope, success, comfort, understanding, reconciliation and joy.

Many of life's trials and hardships are the result of misunderstandings, or being unable to see things in their proper perspective, and Dag is the symbol of the promise that everything will eventually become clear in the end.

Specifically, Dag represents a victory of sorts that is non-confrontational or violent. Unless combined with power runes, such as Sig or Tyr, Dag may suggest that the solution to any trouble or task in hand will best be achieved by using your powers of understanding and a non-aggressive outlook.

The final and successful completion of any task or project is often foretold by Dag, or perhaps a lasting reconciliation between quarrellers.

Dag represents the joy of new beginnings and new days. You are able to look forward with optimism, as well as looking back with understanding.

People represented by Dag are usually honest, cheerful and optimistic people.

The 'and they all lived happily ever after' rune is generally a good rune for magic, adding a little sun to a lot of situations, but particularly for desired conclusions.

In many ways, Dag is the more passive form of sig, where your victory is the realisation that the monsters around you are flowers and trees, or even friends. Dag is the coming to terms with things rune. Like Yr, Dag is a good rune for people troubled by anxiety. In magic, Dag can be used to dispel fears and end strife. Particularly if you have fears that you suspect are better viewed head on, Dag is your friend.

Probably the mellowest rune, Dag might be a suitable charm for those who wish to focus on the brighter side of life.

This cheery rune would probably be my first choice as a starting point for those who want to try meditation involving the runes. Witnessing a sunrise is an obvious time and location for this.

To my knowledge, the only instance on which I would avoid Dag is with the possibly terminally ill or doomed. If the only way out is a severe one, Dag could hasten this (albeit rarely). Yrr or Niet and Dag do not easily combine well, as a result.

Like Ansur, Dag is a poor guardian of secrets, but in a good way.

# Extra Runes for the Anglo-Saxon Futhork

These extra runes are presented here mostly because of The Anglo-Saxon Rune Poem, which has been used throughout my descriptions of the Elder Futhark. I do not personally use them with my readings or rune sets. However, I feel that the complete omission on my part of these extra runes would deny the reader the ability to read the poem as it is. It would also deny the reader the ability to see the entire cosmology of the poem itself, which is valid too in its own way. It may be that you choose to add these extra runes into your own set, but even if you don't, it may be useful to know about these extra runes, as you may be able to see where they represent ideals already present in the Elder Futhark, and yet not really embellished in the Poem itself.

The extra runes of the Anglo Saxon 'Futhork' (the set has a different name) were probably introduced by the Saxons and Frisians. As their languages changed, a need for more phonetic symbols rose, and thus these extra runes and variants appeared.

*The Anglo-Saxon Rune Poem* is alone in its description of these extra runes as magical symbols. It actually appears to be the oldest surviving rune poem, although we do not know this for sure. Sadly, the original manuscript was lost in the Great Fire of London.

The *Anglo-Saxon Rune Poem* is definitely the easiest to read, as it has the most obvious structure, as well as a clear relationship to all of the twenty four major runes of the Elder Futhark.

Having said this, the Elder Futhark has what I believe to be a complete cosmology, or universal understanding already contained, and I personally believe that these extra runes only add confusion.

See if you can find ways of expressing these concepts using runes from the Elder Futhark, perhaps alone, or perhaps in combination. If you wish to use Anglo-Saxon runes, I'd recommend further research out-with this book.

Choosing to read with these Anglo-Saxon runes included might need a re-evaluation of Elder Futhark runes to re-balance readings. You will see that some symbols are even swapped. You would need specifically to research this yourself. The Elder Futhark is by far the most popular divination choice, so books on Anglo-Saxon divination are scarce. You are likely to need to lean on historical and archaeological sources, as well as intuition.

I would also argue that they do not generally lend themselves to divination as the Elder Futhark runes do. Many of these runes appear to represent things so odd or drastic as to be unlikely to give fair representation of life patterns with a one in thirty chance of appearing. On a day to day basis your chances at death are not one in thirty, as a rather crude example. If you know what I mean, as a statistician, something that bad would need a heap of relevant runes shouting out at once.

You will notice that the Anglo-Saxon runes continue a little after the poem has ended. I have also chosen a few Anglo-Saxon runes that are even omitted from the poem. These are here to give you what I consider to be a fair representation of the full Anglo-Saxon Futhork as it is more often seen. These are extra runes that I consider common enough in historical finds and Anglo-Saxon writings to be worth considering. From what I know, this gives you what is considered the full Futhork.

Some of these extra runes are also present in Younger Futhark systems and the modern meanings are likely to have been gleaned from here. Some have clues in the names, which can be traced to root words using etymology. Some are also possibly bindrunes, or combinations of other runes, so we can usually glean a degree of their portent. Generally, however, there is less to work with, so tread

with caution. Tread with caution, and treat my descriptions
sceptically.

A degree in Scandinavian studies or Anglo-Saxon language and
culture may prove handy if you are dead set on understanding and
using them.

## Ac

ᚪ

*The oak fattens the flesh of pigs for the children of men.*
*Often it traverses the gannet's bath,*
*and the ocean proves whether the oak keeps faith*
*in honourable fashion.*

Spells: 'a' as in 'ark' or 'aardvark'

Ac represents the oak and is a fertility rune, representing
sustenance from nature and growth. We can extrapolate that the
formidable majesty of the oak is reflected also.

The poem's mention of a tendency to seaward journeys could
hint at boat building. Oak is a strong and dependable wood, on
which seaward journeys can be embarked.

Its acorns were also fed to livestock in the Middle Ages,
particularly pigs.

Again, nature provides.

As an aside, please note the sea's description as 'gannets bath'.
This is a particularly beautiful example of a 'kenning' (a concept
which will be explored later).

# Aesc

ᚠ

*The ash is exceedingly high and precious to men.*
*With its sturdy trunk it offers a stubborn resistance,*
*though attacked by many a man.*

Spells: 'a' as in 'ash' or 'axe'

The ash is described in myth as the wood that men (as in males) were carved out of by the gods, and thus the ash may symbolise man as the individual. In this story women are carved from elm.

So, Aesc represents humanity, but possibly humanity with regards to the individual, as opposed to the mouth. Its similarity to Ansur hints at intelligence. As a wood, ash has the combined merits of being both useful and magical. Household implements such as brooms and specifically the handles of every day tools were commonly made of ash, as it has a tendency not to splinter. It is also said that the brooms on which witches travelled were made of ash. Ash is a very conductive wood, making the tree a frequent victim of thunder strikes, but also making ash a useful material if you fancy trying a staff or a wand.

Irritatingly, Aesc is visually represented by what in all other rune systems is the rune 'Ansur'. If you want to use the Anglo Saxon runes you will need to swap this rune with Ansur thus:

'Ansur' becomes 'Oss' and looks like this ᚩ

ᚠ becomes "Aesc" and means the above.

Confusing, I know.

Some believe that Yggdrasil was an ash tree, and not a yew. That Aesc is identical to Ansur possibly hints that the divine connection with Odin is not entirely lost.

# Yrr

ᚻ

*Yrr is a source of joy and honour to every prince and knight;*
*it looks well on a horse and is a reliable equipment for a journey.*

Spells: Soft 'y' as in 'yolk'

Quite what literally Yrr depicts is not entirely clear, but practitioners most frequently site the shield. This makes Yrr is a protection rune, but possibly a less restrictive form of protection than Iss or Stan.

Another less likely option is the bow, as well as the saddle or cloak.

Maybe some degree of honour can be attached to Yrr, because of its association with the nobility, which is the one clear thing that the poem states.

As ever, I can see the potential for magical use here but I gladly discount it from readings.

# Io

ᛡ

*Iar is a river fish and yet it always feeds on land;*
*it has a fair abode encompassed by water, where it lives in happiness.*

Spells: 'I' or 'y' as in 'happy' or 'igloo' or 'yodel'

Io is another Anglo-Saxon rune that actually contradicts an elder rune. Identical to the Old Norse depiction of Hagal, which is particularly prevalent in Younger Futharks found in Scandinavia, Io is generally thought to be Iormungard, the world serpent, and thus represents secrets best left untouched.

That the poem has such a benevolent and happy description for the serpent nemesis of Thor strikes me as odd, but not entirely unbelievable, or indeed unique. The African river serpent NyamiNyami is a similar mixture of blessing and danger, as are the mermaids of Europe.

As a note on the pronunciation, in most European languages there's a bit of fun with the 'I', 'g', 'j', and 'y' sounds, hence names like 'John' becoming 'Ian' in Scotland and Jacob becoming 'Yakov' in Eastern Europe. So wherever you see 'I','j',or 'g' in this book, insert some allowances for confusion.

# Ear

*The grave is horrible to every knight,*
*when the corpse quickly begins to cool*
*and is laid in the bosom of the dark earth.*
*Prosperity declines, happiness passes away*
*and covenants are broken.*

Spells: 'ee' as in 'ear', 'seek, or 'eerie'

Ear represents death and the grave. Obviously, this could be abstracted into endings or even new beginnings much in the way that the tarot card of Death is, but still I feel that with the presence of Yr and Dag, Ear skews the set for divination purposes.

This goes a long way towards explaining why I do not use the Anglo-Saxon Futhork.

A sobering image of death neither noble nor fair is presented in this poem. I should state that I feel that the rune itself rather embodies an honour and a progress that these sentiments do not echo. The grave represents the remembering of the dead, as well as an appeal to the gods for safe passage to something better. This sobering image of death is not unique in the ancient world, however.

## Qweordh

Spells: 'qu' or 'kw' as in 'quick' or 'question'

Qweordh is the fire wheel, and its similarity to the swastika places it as a solar entity, emphasising the cyclic nature of the sun.

There is also talk among other practitioners of it symbolising fire in ritual, as the messenger between the physical and spiritual worlds.

## Kalc

Spells: 'k' as in 'kick' or 'cat'

Kalc is a confusing addition to the runes in almost every way. It is also present in Norse Scripts, where it more commonly represents the 'arr' noise (think pirates), but in Anglo-Saxon it is always another 'k'. Runic practitioners generally read it as the symbol of aggressive masculinity and destruction. One thing that this meaning offers is a completely different way to inverse Eohl. What could be the lack of intuition and a guardian angel becomes the ability to rise or stoop to great brutality, and the ability and risk of destruction. It is often likened to the penis, reminding me of toilet walls and the giant figure at Cerne Abbas. Here the humble willy becomes a symbol of threat and not of love or pleasure.

That adding a circle gives you the CND logo is a rather painfully accurate, if unintentional irony. I always feel a touch irked when people write 'peace' or 'love' under a sign that is so blatantly an emblem of how far from peace or love man can stray.

I have also seen this used as shorthand for time of death in medieval records or monuments.

Obviously in a rune set it's 'similarity' to Eohl reversed would make it's presence almost equivalent to a 'bonus Eohl', which is yet another reason that I have for sticking to the Elder Futhark for readings.

## Stan

Spells: 'st' as in 'stone' or 'cast'

Stan means stone and is somewhat like a more concrete or pleasant version of Iss. At least in spell casting, Stan has its place as a protector - particularly as pictorially it lends itself so strongly to the concept.

It also lacks the degree of treachery and slippery danger that Iss contains to an extent, as well as the visionary. This makes it a very specific protection rune.

# Gar

Spells: hard 'g' as in 'gold' or 'gate'

Gar looks like a bindrune of Gyfu and Ing. The word 'bindrune' is used for multiple runes combined to create a single more complex form, and this concept is explained later. It is generally agreed that Gar represents Odin's spear. Its esoteric meaning points literally to magic, or the holy. Within Gar are ideas that are already present in Ing, although one interesting feature of this rune was pointed out to me many years ago — it is symmetrical on all axes, which is strange for something dubbed spear. This could be taken to symbolise that magic is a double-edged sword, and that what people send out mystically, they can expect to receive in return.

So while it is not a rune that I use, its message is one that I adhere to.

Interestingly, many rune spells and passages are margined by a chain of Ings, which also creates a bindrune of Gyfu and Ing.

Also noteworthy, the name for garlic literally means 'like gar', or 'like magic'. We now know how healthy garlic is as a source of important nutrients, and an immunity booster, but in ancient times garlic was thought of as literally a dispeller of evil, just like the vampire movies.

# Ken

Spells: 'k' as in 'kick' or 'cat'

Ken is a common variant of Kaon and, were you to use it, it would replace Kaon entirely. This variant is not specific to Anglo-Saxon Futhork, and also features in some of the Norse Younger

Futharks. However, in the later Norse runic poetry it's meaning changes to 'cist' or 'absess', bringing a whole rune dedicated to disease onto the table. Note that the Anglo-Saxon poem retains the traditional torch meaning despite the fact that the Anglo-Saxons frequently used this other form.

# Using the Runes

*"Know how to cut them, know how to read them,*
*Know how to stain them, know how to prove them,*
*Know how to evoke them, know how to score them,*
*Know how to send them, know how to send them"*

If you have been reading this book from the start, I imagine that by now you will already have some idea of what the Runes are about, and whether or not you are going to benefit from this knowledge. You may even be beginning to see how — if at all — they fit into your own current personal beliefs, and indeed you may even be re-formulating your ideas. However, so far all that has been given is raw knowledge. This section goes into the idea (if not necessarily the truth) of the wisdom of the Runes.

When I first discovered the Runes as an adolescent of about thirteen years of age, I was hooked immediately and was able to learn all of the Runes and their names almost instantly. Having learned these basics with ease, I felt like a magical grand master back then — but I am now still learning about how Rune knowledge can be applied wisely, and I feel that I am not likely to ever be convinced that I truly know as much as I'd like to.

The feeling you get when you start to know all of the names and literal meanings of the various Runes is great, but only through repeated use and contemplation do we get anywhere near understanding their true natures, and maybe more importantly their nature with regards to ourselves.

Now, I'll introduce you to as many of the methods and uses of the Runes as I can, as well as the ideologies and setbacks most strongly associated with them.

# Reading the Runes

## *What you'll need*

Rune readings require little in terms of equipment, and setting yourself up needn't cost you much.

To start with, you are going to need your own rune set, which can be bought ready-made from most large bookshops — although eventually you are better making them yourself.

You'll also need a special pouch or purse for them, with a top that fastens or ties to keep them safe while you are travelling, although a box may do for the home.

Some rune users also have ritual cloths or rugs upon which reading and magic are conducted on.

These are helpful, but not necessary, unless you want to use them as guides for spreads or the casting.

If you wish to do so, I recommend buying a plain piece of fabric that you like, and either drawing (with permanent or fabric pens) or sewing any information upon it that you need.

# 'Carving' your Runes

For carving your runes, you'll need 24 identical or similar objects that you can carve, cut, paint, or draw your runes on to. Most people opt to use wood or stone, but really the choice is yours.

Traditionally the Runes are carved from a freshly cut branch from a fruit bearing tree, ash, birch, or yew.

This possibly sounds more daunting than it is. A stick sliced like a loaf of bread gives you many beads that can have runes carved or burned into them.

All fruiting trees are considered good for rune charms, but the harder woods are more practical, as they smooth up better and splinter less. Call me a hippy, but I only take dead wood, and ask the tree first.

One very practical caveat to remember is that once you've lost one rune, then that set might be done-for. This means that making your runes out of something replaceable to start with might be a wise choice. You may want to carry them everywhere with you. You might lose one. My personal long term set is yew wood, but I have used sticks, dominoes, clay, smoothed coins, dismantled wind ornaments and lolly-sticks — and they have all been fine. In fact, a very powerful set was made in thirty minutes with snapped sticks and a Biro pen. It was very ugly, and worked perfectly.

Interestingly, one of the earliest descriptions of fortune telling, which appears in Julius Caesar's *Gallica*, describes the druids as carving angular signs onto freshly cut branches and casting them like lots. Many believe this to be an early description of the Runes.

You don't need to be a great artist to make your runes, but they should at least be recognisable, and roughly symmetrical where applicable.

Carving or inscribing is the best way to mark your runes, but don't worry if you can't. As long as the runes don't wear off, drawing will do.

Another option is to use heated metal from a fire or gas cooker to burn them into wood, although this could be dangerous.

Your runes, however, should be and feel special to you. They are sacred objects, so no picking your teeth with them, or playing tiddlywinks.

You should also be aware that various rune users draw the runes differently. I have tried to provide the variations within the *Meanings of the Runes* section. I'd recommend making sure you keep to one set traditional arrangement, but at the end of the day it's up to you.

As you become better versed in both using and making runes, you may find meditation beforehand a useful way to validate your rune set.

## *Making Your Pouch*

Small sealable pouches are readily available and cheap in most alternative clothes shops and mystical shops. But, should you choose to make your own pouch, it's quite easy to do so, and if you're not too ambitious, it shouldn't take longer than half an hour.

You will need a square of fabric in any colour, large enough to wrap them in, a needle and thread, and a bit of nice string, chord or ribbon.

Cut out a square a bit more than twice as wide as you're going to need the bag to be, and about one-and-a-half times as long.

Place your chord, ribbon or string on the side that you want on the inside at the top, fold the fabric down over it and sew it down.

Fold it in half along its width with the sewn down hem on the outside. Now is the time when you may decide to decorate your pouch - many people have the Rune Eohll sown into their pouch, to protect their runes.

Now stitch along the edges of the corner and open side of your folded fabric. Stitch carefully, or you may lose runes later.

Now cut off any excess fabric and turn it inside out and you now have your rune pouch, ready to use.

The chord lets you tie your pouch shut, and I use it to fasten my runes to my trousers.

# Preparing Yourself

Before you begin trying your own readings, you would be wise to re-read this following section, as although a lot of it is fairly simple stuff, it's important to get it right.

Whilst it is acceptable to use the Runes for fun, respect and consideration are advised. Many practitioners believe that some questions can only be asked once and if you're unsatisfied with the way that you did these readings you may end up regretting it. Always remember that flustered readings are bad readings.

# A Good State of Mind

If you know you're going to do readings, don't get drunk or stoned unless that's actually an integral part of what you're investigating.

In my experience, drugs slow you down mentally — and this applies to stimulant drugs also. Drugs tend to do as much temporary damage to your intuition as they do to your other mental abilities. You need to be able to focus on the Runes, and remain untainted, which is difficult enough sober, let alone when you are 'away with the fairies'.

Many people promote various rituals to help the rune reader clear their mind, and these are valid. If you're experienced in meditation, this may be an option.

All practitioners recommend spending a while relaxing before you read. This allows you to leave behind whatever frame of mind the previous twenty-four hours has given you — at least as well as you can.

This is important because if your moods are swayed in a certain direction, the Runes will, more than likely, take on at least an element of this sway and so lose accuracy. In other words, a miserable reader will more than likely get a miserable reading, and an elated reader will most often get an elated reading.

You don't necessarily have to be reeling with joy, overwhelmed with power, or calm to the point of stupor — but try to at least get to a stable state of mind.

## *Your Purpose and Technique*

What do you want to know?

It is important when fortune telling with the Runes to have a definite idea of what you want.

If you're asking specific questions, take care to have a definitive idea of what the question really is. Re-phrase it a few times to yourself to ensure you're totally clear as to what you want to know.

Try also to ask questions in a positive way. This is not because negativity is a bad idea, but more because logical problems that can occur when reading the results later, particularly when using the simpler readings wherein each rune is fundamentally important.

Many simpler questions might be seeking a simple yes or no, but when you ask "Am I going to have a crap day", or "Is my so-called friend a nasty piece of work?", you're confronted with a problem when reading the answer. This is because the Runes won't necessarily give yes or no answers. The Runes do have positive or negative values that could be construed as yes or no, but their primary value is of a symbolic nature. Choosing a negatively phrased question can leave you with some awkward logical questions. You have to decide whether positive runes are saying, "Yes, you're right", or "No, this is good".

Badly asked questions usually get confused answers, and it is well worth taking time to figure out exactly what you mean before starting.

How will you choose your Runes?

Over time, people have used a variety of methods for choosing their Runes when they are doing a reading.

Some people pick their runes directly out of their pouch, one by one, and place them appropriately, until all their runes are in place. Others cast all of their runes on the floor and then, mixing them constantly and facing the sky, pick out their runes from the floor. This method is the messiest, and you may lose your runes from time to time, but it's my preferred method, particularly if you can afford to splash out on a nice piece of material to shuffle them on.

## *Placing the Runes*

Always try to have in your mind a clear idea of which method or spread you are going to use.

If you are going to devise your own custom-spread, what does your allocated order of spots, or "houses", represent? Write it down, as you will forget (trust me), and saying "This rune represents your family ... erm ... I think" is not going to satisfy you, or anyone else.

Are you going to take the Runes out of your questioner's hands, or are they going to place them themselves?

If you are reading runes that another person has chosen, make sure you both agree which way up they are. My advice here is to ask them to hold each one up — as if to look at it — and take the rune from them at this point.

Whatever method you choose, to avoid confusion, make sure you decide which way up you have them before placing them. Nothing wrecks a reading like a rune on its side. You will be asking: is it reversed, or upright?

This may sound obvious, but it can really stump you. The Runes are confusing enough without you still needing to decide what way round they all are, and where to place them.

# Methods of Reading

## *The Easiest Way (Spreads)*

The easiest way to read the Runes is by using spreads. This means after choosing your runes, you lay them out on a chart of some description which indicates places or "houses", which represent a pre-defined aspect of your reading.

Then each rune can be read as the representative of whatever aspect it is placed on. So, for instance, if you have a place representing 'love-life', the rune on that place represents how your love life is going.

The simplest reading of this sort is to choose just one rune, and have it represent whatever you like.

The questioner asks their question, and then picks a single rune.

This reading is not advised for questions that require complicated answers.

## *The Three Norns*

The Three Norns is regarded by many as the most ancient and authentic runic spread. This spread's name is derived from the three holy sisters who are said to decide the fate of the world.

The Three Norns method involves picking three signs and laying them left to right.

# The Three Norns

The first rune, 'Urd' (pronounced like lemon curd, or a herd of sheep), represents the eldest sister of the same name and thus reads as past influences. These are events in the past that led to the status of the issue in hand.

The second rune position, named 'Nerthandr' or 'Verdandi', is represented by the motherly middle sister, who symbolises the present. This rune reveals the current status of the subject in question or — if you haven't defined a set subject for this reading — this rune will help you decipher what the subject of this reading is.

Finally, the third rune, 'Skuld', is for the youngest sister, who decides our future.

This rune shows the most likely outcome of events, and suggests whether you should you continue with your current plan, or lack of plan.

### The Celtic Cross

The Celtic Cross is basically nabbed from the Tarot system, where it was originally developed, but is a useful pre-defined pattern if you want a general reading -

most people agree that it encompasses enough, at least, for a general fortune telling session.

Rather than trying to fit the questioner's entire life into a reading, the Celtic Cross nearly always focuses on one or two aspects. You can ask questions to an extent — but the subject matter is generally chosen by the Runes themselves.

Many rune practitioners recommend this method, although interpretations can vary.

There are a few variations of this spread, but it generally consists of ten houses representing the following:

1. You.
2. The challenge or the issue at hand.
3. The origin or root of the Issue.
4. The more recent past.
5. The actual moment.
6. What will happen immediately next.
7. Your attitudes.
8. Your environment.
9. Your hopes and fears.
10. The outcome.

The first house represents you, or the person that is having the reading. It may hint at the underlying make up or traits of the reader, or their needs as a person with regards to the situation that is about to unfold. This is not to be confused with their direct hopes or fears regarding the issue, or their current attitudes which are dealt with later. This house represents what they initially brought to the table by just being what they are.

The second house represents the issue that the reading concerns. It is the rune in this house that defines what the whole reading is dealing with. Where this rune is positive, it can be seen as an aspiration or need to reach the positive state described; where the rune is negative, it shows the main problem, threat, or weakness that the questioner is to consider in this reading.

The third house suggests the events that lead up to the current situations, or important past influences. Sometimes the rune here provides useful background information if you're reading for someone else.

Celtic Cross Spread

The fourth house represents events as yet unseen, or unrealised — events that are going to influence the final result.

The fifth house represents the questioner's desired outcome.

The sixth house gives advice, things that the questioner should know, and possible actions or inaction that will be for the general good.

The seventh house represents the questioner's attitudes. In other words, this rune indicates how exactly the questioner feels about the situation in hand, and how they are dealing with it as a person. In conjunction with the houses dealing with environment and advice, this is useful to see how their perceived situation and method compares to the actual situation - and the best way forward.

The eighth house reveals the environment, or what's going on around the questioner that is either helping or hindering them.

The ninth house refers to the hopes or fears of the questioner. A rune with a positive aspect is likely to represent the eventual outcome that the questioner wishes for with regards to the issue in hand, whereas negative runes should be read as fears. These hopes and fears may be yet more hints at attitudes that are either helpful, or harmful. In this way, important clues as to behaviours, expectations and remedies may lurk in this seemingly ethereal house.

The tenth house is the outcome. Interestingly (and often comfortingly), the general belief is that these readings have a lifespan of somewhere between six and eighteen months, so if it's overwhelmingly gloomy, don't lose too much sleep over it.

Finally, a beneficial custom is to turn all of the reversed runes upright, and then focus on how they can improve their outlook by taking on the virtues of these more positive runes. The Celtic Cross, and indeed most spread-based fortune telling methods, are not fatalistic and merely show where current trends are leading. So, at the end of a particularly grim reading, it is often good to show how these dark tidings can be turned and used to make a more positive future. Of course, some runes such as Yr and Iss cannot be turned — but where this is true it is still possible to pull out positive feedback for the questioner.

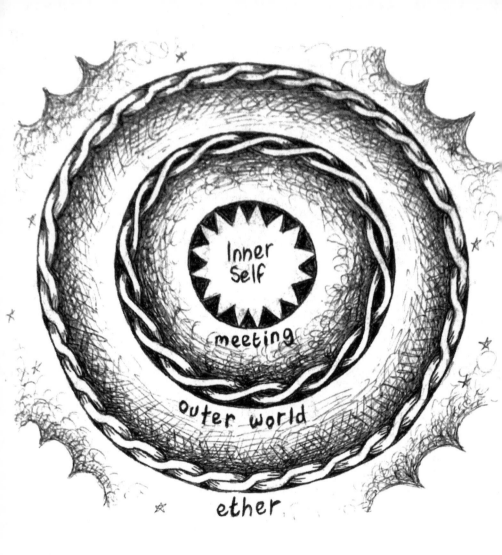

Inner
Self

meeting

outer world

ether

circles of
Perception

# The Hardest Way (Casting)

This method is probably my favourite, as it lets the Runes decide everything.

It also feels great.

However, this method does require a lot of practise, intuition, and knowledge of the Runes. Even when you're adept, you'll still need to sometimes admit that you don't know what's going on within this reading method, because it can be very confusing.

To carry out this style of reading, you either take all of the runes, or choose nine runes (by scrabbling inside your pouch, or rune container), and them cast them onto the floor.

Then, you can just read them as they lie, without any help — although you can also devise large tables, which can help.

A common table is a table of three circles; the inner wheel representing you, the second ring representing the physical or seen world, and the outer ring representing the spiritual world, or the unseen.

Runes lying outside the outer circle are often discarded, and the runes lying on the boundaries are read as events either entering your physical world from the spiritual, or events from the real world confronting you, depending on which boundary they lie.

Other than that, instead of the runes having their meanings defined by 'houses' the runes become significant by means of relation to each other. For example: are they opposing, are they near each other, or are they forming a string?

I should stress that the circular diagram above is there to help, and not obligatory. Many of my own more interesting readings have had no diagrams involved at all.

# Your Own Way

If you can think of better ways of using the Runes, try them out!

You may have names for houses or areas that are more relevant to your needs, or you may feel uncomfortable with certain aspects of a spread, or not understand it.

Most 'magical' spreads are chosen and used not for their divine significance, but for their ease of use and relevance.

Many practitioners will explain to you that their chosen system echoes the structure of the universe, or relates to some sacred image or symbol, but in truth, they often just like it.

Trust me — very little is known about genuine mystical spreads and reading methods from Europe, so your guess is at least as good as the Victorians, or hippies, who probably made up most of the common rune reading systems you see today.

## *Help*

Hopefully, your intuition will be able to guide you through most of your readings, as I have tried to present as much information as you'll need to start reading for yourself and your friends. However, these further hints may help you when doing readings.

When you can't make sense of the runes, or the results seem irrelevant, or vague, try this: think of what they don't mean. If the Runes had a better way of telling you the message you're currently pursuing, they would have done it.

Also, why not look at the runes that aren't there?

For instance, why might you get Lagu (the sea), and Rad (the sun-wheel), and not Eh (the Horse) in your reading? Well, here you've got two runes which suggest travel, but Eh represents travelling amongst friends, and that they will be of consequence. In this way, Eh's lacking may suggest that this journey will be the focus of your own change, and that it will happen unaided or unhindered.

This may seem complicated, but it will help you if you're completely stuck.

Also, If you've asked a 'yes or 'no' question, don't expect a 'yes' or 'no' answer — nor even a 'maybe', necessarily. The Runes are much more likely to be presenting you with information in the form of symbolism than they are with a simple positive or negative value — so always concentrate on their meaning first.

In fact, while it is important to get to know which runes have a more generally positive meaning than others, their values to this effect are far less important than their symbolic meanings, which are the key players in helping you construct meaningful arguments and narratives.

As an example, if you were considering a camping trip and asked the Runes whether it was a good idea, water runes such as 'Lagu' or 'Ing' may well represent rain — even though they are very positive signs.

You may also sometimes be confronted by readings that don't seem to fit with what you perceive to be the truth. My advice here is to keep your own opinions until afterwards, and then express your personal feelings later if you feel the need. As a fortune teller, you will be more respected for this — and always remember that what you see, is not necessarily what is.

When in doubt, write your reading down somewhere. You may look back at this and have a "Eureka!" moment that will prove useful at a later date.

As well as this, recording your reading is actually a good idea anyway. Not only does it mean that you can refer to them at a later date, and compare them with what actually happened, but it also shows how you're progressing, as well as providing an aid to your memory.

Finally, don't be coy about using books. There is a lot to memorise about the Runes, and you'll never stop learning from others. I still consult several books at home, as well as all of the relevant ancient texts that I can get my hands on. I find that different people's perspectives gives greater insights.

No one on entering the fortune-teller's caravan wants or expects the reader to reach out for their Fortune Telling for Beginners guidebook mid-reading — but at the same time, if you've stopped learning, you haven't learned enough.

# Rune Magic

This chapter marks a turning point in this book. Until this point belief in anything has not been needed, and hopefully hasn't been thrust upon you; but magic is magic, and here we delve into huge leaps of faith by merely mentioning the word.

If you consider magic either evil or nonsense, it is with caution that I urge you to continue reading. More clues as to what the Runes actually are or were will be found, and possibly the odd interesting anecdote, but the dogmatic Skeptic or the overly superstitious may find little more of interest here.

As already stated, there are plenty of reasons why reading the Runes may be enlightening or at least fun for everyone. Meditating and casting spells with them is likely to be pointless to someone who does not believe in magic. At the very best you will be proved wrong, which is usually an unpleasant experience. Even to those that love it, magic is many things, but easy, rewarding and safe are not always on the shopping list.

Neither is magic popular. Witches are no longer dragged into the streets and burned where I live, but between the sceptics that view you as charlatan and the superstitious that brand you as evil, or 'spooky', there are plenty of situations that do not welcome the mystic. Particularly the novice or self proclaimed mystic.

So, if what you wanted was fun, you now have it. I advise you to skip to the section on the gods, and possibly to the section on literally reading the Runes on ancient monuments etc. And the appendices, which in this book are almost another book in their own right.

If, after reading the above, you still want to pursue rune magic actively, and are even considering making this magic a feature of your life, read on.

The Runes as a magical system are different from most other mystical systems that survive in Europe. They were not invented to work either along-side, or in response to the magical systems connected to Judaism, Christianity, or Islam. Thus, rune magic should be seen as a separate practice, existing aside many of the other forms of magic used in western society.

Many systems that originated in Europe for example rely on either the Kabbalistic teachings of the ancient Hebrew faith, or the teachings of related mystical groups, such as the Rosicrucian Order, The Golden Dawn, The Knights Templar, and others. This strong reliance on these Gnostic paths is largely because of the information vacuum caused by the forbidden nature of the original practices, along with an understandable unwillingness of the original users of these systems to share their knowledge. This means that in some cases the true meanings and uses of these systems have now been either as good as lost, or diluted to beyond the point of perception.

To clarify, it is not that there is anything particularly wrong with Kabbalism, but Kabbalistic and Gnostic systems are not traditionally Pagan, and are fundamentally based on theories that are not present in the Runes.

On the other hand, some of this stuff might seem a bit obvious. That is because many of us are either culturally or literally descended from these people, and much of what we now hold as given was developed therein. Then there is commonality where either that literally is the truth, or that is what people tended to think. You will have to forgive the odd cliché. As an obvious example, when a child is asked to draw Merlin, they will invariably draw a two-eyed Odin. Wizard's garb is at least shared in northern culture, if not descended from it. Obviously, it is hoped that a true context and meaning of these traditions will help you see them anew.

Where are we going with all of this? I feel the need to warn you that what you are now going to get is quite minimal, because I want to keep it clean, and by clean I mean genuinely runic, genuinely universal, or based on what I have found to work. It is also not guaranteed to be either glamorous or exotic, but again it is hopefully authentic.

## Does it work?

The simple answer to that very complex question is "Often".

In a purely scientific manner, there are a few very important reasons why it is hard to tell.

For a start, the placebo effect is pretty incredible, and giving a blessing really does work even if the underlying system is inherently wrong. A good example of this is that when they test drugs on cattle - not only do they need to have a fake test to compare with, but they need to hold back the information of who gets the real pill from the farmers. Cows that are fed by farmers who believe that they are getting treatment do better than cows that don't regardless of the actual treatment.

As an anecdote, I once worked with an acupuncturist who had to discount quite ridiculously positive statistics on this basis. He was curing people of drug addiction in figures that more than doubled conventional methods, but was aware of how strong the placebo effect was in his work, which sadly did not lend it self to a fair blank comparison. In presenting his product I was not allowed to share his statistics for this reason.

Placebo is actually real enough to be a pain in the neck for the mystic who genuinely wants to know that all of their work is indeed of ethereal merit. We shall explore this problem in great depth later on.

Of course, this placebo effect and the power of suggestion are plenty for the sceptical to play with. Part of me feels that if it works then the result is what matters. If I could bottle the placebo effect I would; honest placebo isn't out of the question.

'Here…this will make you feel better, and feeling better is proven to increase your likelihood of getting better.'

In this way the rune magic directed at inner goals could be seen as a way of focussing your mind and tuning attitudes in regards to one's needs or personal growth, regardless of your belief system. Giving thoughts and needs a name, and then even wearing them around our necks, is a valid activity for a sceptic. In daily life we can lose this connection and we can also set ourselves harmful or negative goals if we are not careful - maybe a lucky charm will keep us in the right direction.

But is rune magic purely placebo?

That is a hard question, but some things hint 'no'. Most people are incredulous, or indeed utter strangers to the idea of the Runes. They generally do not know what to expect, and these people do not seem unaffected. So, in short, generally results exceed expectations. My personal spell casting doesn't reach a large enough mass for me to say anything awe inspiring, and sometimes nothing does indeed happen gloriously, but enough happens to keep it valid.

It should definitely be stated here that I am not a millionaire, and do not have everything that I could possibly want. Neither am I deliriously happy all of them time. There are plenty of mystics out there who do not have all that they want either inside or out. That definitely isn't how it works.

One thing of note is that blessing others usually goes better than blessing yourself in almost every way imaginable, which 'fiddles the book' somewhat. Somehow wishing for cake is nowhere near as effective as wishing that someone else has a cake. I have observed this first hand but have also frequently heard this noted by others.

Active magic is also hard, it does go wrong, and when it goes right you are still left with whatever new strain of destiny you have unfolded with it. Also note that magic is largely frowned upon by the general public. If you have got this far, and are still keen, you are in the minority. That it is equally frowned upon by both the sceptical and the superstitious is something worth being aware of. People who declare themselves as magical are not selling themselves to the general public.

The belief that the Runes are magical also does not negate the idea that the above belief or lack of belief in either yourself or those around you cannot work against you. If nothing else, you will need a degree of faith and self-control to even try the more *magical* experiences. One the underlying principles of magic, is that we are all doing *magic* all of the time whether we want to or not. In this way, your willful magic is sometimes a drop in the ocean.

# Magical Tools

There is evidence of magical tools being used by man that goes back as far as we have been able to stretch our knowledge.

From talismans of protection such as amulets and bells to ritual tools such as wands, torches and sacred objects, the path of the seer and magician has been littered with artefacts of power.

None of these objects are strictly necessary in their own right, but they all have their place as magical aids.

For the larger part, their role is to aid you in visualising your set purpose, although don't underestimate the benefits of things feeling and looking authentic.

Your priest or original American shaman is using his own awe and that of his viewers to reach the spirit-world as much as anything else when he dances, chants, and gesticulates with his psychic tools. This is not charlatanism, it is getting the ball rolling.

As a rune user, there are many tools that can aid your spiritual quests, which are briefly described in the following section.

## Holy Stuff

If you're really serious about magic you may consider wearing clothes that get you in the place.

I personally have this down to taste. Some of us really benefit from props or attire that lend to the event, and help us to feel connected. Some of us would just feel silly.

It feels strange to say that these opposing tendencies are both right, but on one hand giving something a facade does not make it fake, and if you do not believe that, feel free to remove all decorations from your life. All clothing is costume, whether it be a branded top, a top hat or a wizard's cloak, and in this way is part of the human experience. As ever, this can be traced back to our cave dwelling ancestors. You should neither feel guilty for needing to don a cape, nor from your favourite pair of tracksuit bottoms or leggings. If you feel wrong, you are wrong; if you feel right, you are right. The Gods do not care what you are wearing and neither should your neighbours.

The only thing that is utterly essential is that what you have and wear does not distract. This means that they mustn't be uncomfortable, embarrassing or annoying you while you work. To this end, I wear black.

Odin is said to have worn a grey cloak, representing the sky. Cloaks are also warm and look the part. Again don't knock looking the part. Any part of ritual as a means to acquiring spiritual connection is as valid as it feels inside.

Blue is also a colour of portent, featuring heavily in Norse saga, where if someone is seen wearing blue, something big is about to happen. In fairness, this may be connected with the challenge of making blue dye - making blue a 'Sunday best' colour. Blue pigment was often over embellished in medieval paintings to establish the wealth of the patron in the viewer's eyes. However its connection with sky and water make it important.

Red is a protecting colour, as evidenced by the customs among both Norse and Celtic peoples with red berries like holly or rowan. The name Rowan, for boys and trees alike, is from Norse and literally means 'red one'. Interestingly, Viking understanding of colour is slightly odd here, as a lot of what we would describe as orangey or even yellow was thought of as 'red'. Actual gold was described as 'red', for instance.

I do not wear a cloak, but am not adverse to it.

Wands are surprisingly useful. They allow you to picture and direct flows and energies. They are solely about directing and projection but work well with runes. Wood from the ash tree is particularly good, being both conductive and soft to the touch.

However, hands are great too.

Drawing runes can help you visualise them, and projecting runes is safer than inscribing them. Attempting to project and move energies is a great way of getting to know both them and your body.

Swords are also used, and spears. This is obviously martial in nature, but not necessarily a commitment to a martial way. I would certainly never want to actually hit someone with a sword, unless it was in play. Swords can certainly help you get some emotions out of your system in an abstract way, although caution should be used. You want to expel them most of the time, or find a better home for them, and take care not to just exercise them. Love and hate are both muscles that you can choose to grow or atrophy.

Wands and swords share the art of dance and gesture, which can be used to revisit ordeal or emotion to better understand it, or positively to psych you into action and extend your limits.

In the earlier section on fortune telling a special cloth is described briefly. These can also be handy for defining holy places, but also for comfort and not losing your stuff. You can add to the splendour of the event by decorating these, but be careful to not get carried away and create a distraction.

## *Holy Times*

There are known time patterns associated strongly with both runes and Norse gods, but before I start, I find mystical calendars and the idea of special magic times questionable. I do know that these special times are real. My experience is, however, that they don't happen for us all on, say, Halloween (I have never had a spiritual Halloween), or the seventh full moon on a Thursday.

Modern astrology is remarkably modern, and the current teachings of the zodiac were largely formulated in the UK in the 1930s. They are based on ancient Assyrian observations passed on by the ancient Egyptians and then the Greeks, but the current methodology as seen in horoscopes is new.

The ancient astrology that we currently use was not designed for individuals, and was not used thus until the *Daily Mirror* began doing so. We do not on the whole understand the planets, and whilst I personally believe that they do influence us hugely, I'm not sure that anybody knows how.

If you are at all like me, you will not be able to choose or predict these magical times in your life, and can do your best by just leaving the door open for them as often as you can.

Having said all of this, however, I'll now try and share what I know, which may prove useful to you.

Time keeping with the Norse way was accurate, surprisingly so, but extremely complex, and sometimes varying hugely from region to region. There are a number of runic almanacs found all over Europe that take the winter solstice as the begging of the year, and count through the year using the Futhark. However, confusingly there are a few variants on the system, and what they largely share is adherence to the lunar cycle over the solar cycle. In many cases these runic correspondences also appear to be numerical, as opposed to symbolic. By this I mean that Feoh frequently means mean 'one' or 'Monday', as opposed to 'wealth' or 'cow' on these almanacs. Continuing this analogy to make it clear, Ur becomes two or Tuesday.

This is ironic as one Pagan tradition that survived in the UK was the weekday names, which happen to align a bit too comfortably with the Roman week-names.

dies Lunae (moon) = Monday (Moon day)
dies Martis (mars) = Tuesday (Tiu's day)
dies Mercurii (Mercury) = Wednesday (Wotan or Odin's day)
dies Iovis (Jupiter) = Thursday (Thor's day)
dies Veneris (Venus) = Friday (Frigga's day)
dies Saturnii (Saturn) = Saturday (so Saturn stayed Saturn)
dies Solis (Sun day) = Sunday

It is interesting here to note that on one hand these people were willing to compare gods of separate cultures like this in the Dark Ages. I have already stated the opinion that Odin and Mercury are fairly dire fits, but this did happen. Another example is that we know that the planet Venus was called Friggjarstjarna , or 'Frigg's star'.

It is, however, likely that the Viking year was different from region to region or even career to career.

I have heard many variants on Viking month names over the years, but one thing that we actually have in terms of a concrete calendar is Snorri Sturlluson's description of months in his *Prose Edda*. It is a lunar system, each month literally starting on the new moon, and runs roughly thus. New moon is traditionally seen as the night of the first sighting of the moon as it reappears on our skies.

Aligning this calendar roughly with our modern calendar, you would start with Hrutmanuthr or 'Ram's Month', which would start on the nearest new moon to Yule.

On the next new moon you would start Thorri, or 'less', which probably reflects food stores running out. Then you have Goi, or 'snow', which would usually start mid February.

Einmanuthr, or 'lone month', starts approximately mid - March.

Interestingly, I've also heard the name 'lenting' used here, which means starving used for this month. This idea name and concept was borrowed by early Christians and translated into a month of voluntary abstinence.

Gaukmanuthr, or 'cuckoo month' follows, and then a month that Snorri provides three names for - 'Eggtid', Sathtid, or 'Stektid' which mean 'egg tide', 'seed tide', or 'lambing pen tide'. Solmanudr or 'sun month' starts on the nearest new moon to the solstice.

Late summer and autumn are punctuated by 'Heyanir', 'CornSkurnarmanuthr' and 'Haustmanuthr'. Heyanir means 'haying', Conskurnarmanuthr means 'Corn reaping month', and Haustmanuthr literally means 'harvest month'.

The year ends with Gormanuthr, or 'blood month', which refers to the slaughtering of livestock, and Frermanuthr, or 'frozen month'.

You will note that these names are largely of a practical nature, and often refer to farming or weather cycles. That these cycles also have a mystical nature is not in question, but they do not particularly heed gods or runes.

I also feel the need to highlight the fact that this is obviously a calendar mapped out for farmers, and not warriors. These people so regularly honoured and scandalised by their violence were largely farmers.

An interesting but rarer rune calendar is the division of the year into runes. This makes each rune approximately a half-month or fortnight of the year, but again I'd see this as inspiration, and not hard and fast fact. If you wish to investigate this idea, the first full moon after yule is used to mark the division between Feoh, and Dag. Whilst I know of no evidence of actual ancient people drawing the full Futhark out in a circle and using this to divide the year into months, it is logical, and weirder still it has worked for me.

One thing that seems clear is that the northern peoples celebrated the solstices, equinoxes, and "eight days" as seasonal markers much as the Celts and Romans did. We also have seasons, which reflect both the light of the sun hitting us, and the annual slumber and awakening of nature, at least in the Northern Hemisphere. This is a commonality that we can trust.

Most of these marker days are still celebrated today, albeit differently, and are now known as follows:

Yule or Christmas, which was sacred to Odin, who is one of the many characters amalgamated into the modern day Father Christmas (hence the flying sledge and reindeer). Yule or 'Yol', as it was originally named, has softened considerably since the dark ages. Yule was a day of judgement, more akin to modern Halloween. The promise of lighter skies was celebrated, but the most desperate times were still ahead. The Santa that now comes bearing gifts, once roared across the skies punishing those that did not celebrate his day. Interestingly, it was the Vikings and Saxons who divided the year by the solstice, for the Celts are believed to have divided the year on Halloween.

'Imbolc' we now think of as the joys of spring, but this marked one the toughest times of year in the ancient north despite the more clement weather. Winter stores are stretched to collapse and summer plenty is still distant in the future. This festival marked a time for tightening your belt, planting your crops and praying that they would grow. Lambs were eagerly and hungrily awaited.

Easter was traditionally a solar festival marking the spring equinox, or the first full moon after, but has been controlled by the Church since the Middle Ages at least. The festival actually gets its name from a little known Saxon goddess 'Ostara'. Little is known about Ostara from any direct source. Notably, Ostara or her Norse equivalent does not feature in the Edda, and there are no stories of her.

I have a fairly wild conjecture that I feel I must share here. I suspect that 'Ostara' may be connected in some way to the distant goddess Isis, or even the Assyrian 'Ishtar'. The Romans took Isis from the Egyptians and spread her name far and wide, despite their not adopting her into the pantheon of now well-known Greco-Roman gods.

Easter marks an important point of spring. This is the time of year in northern Europe where things aren't just beginning to grow, but are beginning to be edible, and thus this festival heralds the end of lean times.

'Mayday' or Beltane celebrates the beginning of summer. Interestingly the Viking year described above was actually ordered as starting roughly a month before this, as the business calendar still does, on April the 1st.

'Midsummer' or the solstice was celebrated as the brightest day. That sounds obvious and I'm pained to write it but that is pretty much all that I have for sure. Celtic, Roman, and even Christian festivals in this case overshadow anything that I have found which could stand out as particularly Runic or Norse. Some say that the Norse god Baldur died on the solstice.

'Lammas' is now a fairly obscure festival, but in terms of Northern tradition it is much better understood. This festival happens in the beginning of August. Lammas celebrates the beginning of the harvest cycle. Strangely it is known as the birth date of Odin, or in Scotland, the death date of "John Barelycorn".

Farmers can now start gathering what they have grown, making this an important time. As an aside, the Scottish tradition of sword dancing on Lammas may be related to the sword dancers recalled by Tacitus in his account of Germany.

The vernal equinox is the latter midpoint between Yule and solstice. It is literally surrounded by traditional festivals, making it hard to pinpoint exactly what was when on a more ancient calendar, but their commonalities are easier to decipher.

'Halloween' in most northern cultures was more strongly connected to the festival of harvest, than the festival of death. This was the time when crops came in and thus a grand measure of both justice and luck for the hands of farmers. It was considered an important spiritual day, but possibly not as ghostly as dark Yule. The harvest festivals in rural Britain are probably closer relatives to this northern festival than our modern spook-fest.

Leaving the solar year behind, we also obviously have the other cycle of day and night. Generally, people agree that the night is a better time to connect with either your inner self or other worlds. However, I suspect that we have this concept due to the quiet and lack of distraction of night-time - not forgetting our fear of and fascination for the dark itself.

Among Wiccans, there is a belief that the waxing moon is good for positive or 'growing' spells, and the waning moon for spells of a dismissing or 'letting go' nature. Nearly all cultures share a belief that the full moon marks a time of great spiritual connection. A neat trick to remember is that the waxing moon follows the cup of your right hand whereas the waning moon cups to the left. Yr is the closest we have to a moon rune. The moon constantly is born, and dies in our skies and yet lives on.

One interesting polar opposite to popular cosmology is that the sun and moon are both represented by female entities, and fairly minor ones at that. Sol and Mani only feature in Norse mythologies as the light-giving maidens pursued by the wolves Skol and Hati.

In this way Norse mythology resembles Assyrian and classical mythology, with major deities representing sky, earth and water more than the solar and lunar bodies.

Of note, lunar and solar eclipses were definitely feared. Later in this book, we will discuss Skol and Hati as a specific Norse legend that relates to eclipses when discussing the gods, but fear of eclipses is world wide and almost universal. If you are going to take the clock and calendar very seriously with regards to magic, this would be a strange choice.

Again I stress that holy times are, at least in my experience, found and defined by events and not calendars. A thunderstorm on a Monday is more thunderous than a mild Thursday, and for me at least, magic has been more like the weather than the clock.

The festivals serve best to create and emphasise community, which is also important. If you are part of a like-minded community, there is a lot to be said for festivals in this way, but my instinct is that as an individual, your magical days will follow their own calendar.

I hope that you, the reader, do not feel that I have taken something from you at this point. It could be felt that I am denying you the magic of special days, or denying you an understanding of the natural harmonies of the earth. That isn't the intention. I'm really just making the case that these holy days are of great cultural importance, but that expecting them to be magical is a bit like expecting snow at Christmas. It doesn't always work out like that. Looking out of your window both literally and metaphorically is usually the best way.

## *Holy Places*

It is no coincidence that religious or mystical places tend to be awesome, and likewise no mistake that the mystic frequently performs in a dramatic manner.

Believing is part of the key to magical procedure, as is feeling the part. The awe that you feel when walking into a church, temple, or Gypsy-caravan plays a large role in your preparation for the mystical experience.

Sadly, there are few Pagan holy places left that are accessible to most of us. Likelihood is that you will have to find your own, and that it will be humbler than it should be. This is a fact that I would love to change.

Whether your place of awe is a stone circle on a windy hill or a warm bath with some nice candles, it is, as ever, your question and your choice. I have personally always leaned to woodlands and trees for my mystical endeavours.

Very importantly, if you have built yourself a set of runes, or indeed obtained them some other way, you already have a portable and potent magical tool which you can use to sanctify an event. Simply encircling yourself with the runes is a simple way to create a hallowed place anywhere.

Likewise, if you have chosen or made yourself a cloth or blanket for your runes you also have a portable pre built sacred place in that.

Music - you can also choose music that you like. Music does much to 'make' a place. There are various musicians that specialise in meditation, but find something that connects with you. Dodgy lyrics are really distracting so instrumental music is often the easy choice.

Possibly what is more important than any location in its own right is your connection to it, which can be grown by simple acts like walking around it, or simply exploring and finding that perfect place.

In some cases runes can be connected to places, which will help you understand them, like Lagu with the sea, or Kaon with a fire, but that is an optional extra.

I consider a comfy spot under a good tree a fine place for meditations and readings, and I am not alone here.

Trees were very important to our ancestors and from the great hall in Beowulf to Valhalla itself, living trees feature as honoured parts of the houses of the grand. That is just the start, however. The formidable Yggdrasil, or tree of life, is sited in Norse mythology as the foundation of everything. The Viking world is a huge rolled up giant bobbing about in an ocean, but the universe is a tree.

# Spells and charms

## *Runes as Magical signs*

Now that we have some backdrop, we can move back to the Runes themselves.

The Runes are most commonly used in magic symbolically, and most of this book deals with the actual symbolic value of the runes. This is not the only way to use the Runes, as will be explained later in this book, but we will now look at how to apply this collection of meanings to magic.

It is not that easy.

For the actual description of the root method, if you imagine making up your ideal rune reading and writing it down as a charm, that is my description.

However, once you have done a few readings and discovered how obtuse many of them can seem, you will quickly realise that your spell can easily go awry. A spell that you write with the intention of passing an exam for example may turn out to be an accidental spell for winning an argument, or even an intense headache.

While worn charms are the most common rune spells, or etchings on prized objects, there are other ways.

Writing a spell on something flammable and burning them adds potency. Most will describe a blue candle (blue for Odin), but I prefer an open hearth.

Blessings drawn directly onto people with finger gestures are also great.

And then there are charms to be given. If you are just beginning, and handing out spells, tell them to give them back if they don't want them. If you destroy them yourself, that's fine. Just throwing them away does not stop them, and if the silly sod burns them, they are rendered more potent.

On a wry note, getting them to return unwanted spells also doubles as a sly way to get them to report the results.

Of note, rune charms were not restricted to holy objects, and were frequently used on practical objects such as tools for protection, luck or even to enhance their efficiency. In archaeological terms, these have been found on weapons, boats, homesteads, tools, jewellery and clothing.

Importantly, the Runes are not from Peter Pan; disbelief doesn't necessarily mean no show. There is also a chance that apparent disbelief is not real disbelief, and you should take that into account.

## Single Rune Charms

An incredible way of visualising a rune is obviously to draw or carve it, and once you're there, you are heading already towards having a single rune charm.

Most people, including myself, settle for talismans or gestures of possibly one or two runes at most. The more runes you use, the more likely you are to be specific, and that tight aim makes them powerful, but on the other hand your chances of making a mistake go up radically, if not exponentially.

Mistakes usually just don't work, but as already hinted at, can actually make things worse, so be careful. I will talk about more complex stuff later, but do not knock the single rune charm. Frequently it is all that you need.

Yes, that single rune on a chain or rope that you might see at new age stalls and alternative bookshops are actually sometimes what is needed, but why not make them yourself.

How to make rune sets has already been described, and making a charm is barely harder. Make rune, drill a hole, get some string, and you have a very pretty pendant and magic tool in one.

I have sometimes carved these on wood as charms or gifts for friends but I often just draw them with gestures for myself or my family.

## *Bind Runes*

The symbol above is a popular bindrune that is said to represent Yggdrasil - the tree of life. In its centre you will find the earth, represented as Ing and Jera. Jera symbolises the cyclic nature of things while Ing represents the earth as the fertile meeting point of many forces. Above, two Eohlls ascend, representing both life and spirituality, but also branches. Interestingly, the roots form Eohll reversed or Calc, which are both negative, but this is a very positive sign, and generally is seen as a blessing, or a key to meaningful meditation.

There are many surviving charms that combine runes making something more specific, and thus more potent. This is an art, and not an easy one. Runes can influence each other in ways that in honesty I am still learning, and in this way I nowadays lean towards caution.

As an example, below is a bindrune form that actually combines all runes. It is usually called 'the mother rune' and is considered fine both as a charm, and as a meditation. However, the fact that a bindrune as simple as this means 'everything that exists' demonstrates how easy it is for a bindrune to mean the wrong thing.

The best I can really do here is provide some bindrune examples.

## Protection

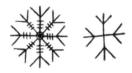

I'll start with these two protection bindrunes.

The more elaborate of the two is quite famous, and claims to be the Aegishjalmir, or 'helm of awe' spell that features in *Havamal*. It first appears in the Icelandic *Galdrbok* in about the 16<sup>th</sup> century. It claims to be a protection for the head, specifically, but its use mainly of the rune Eohll in a protecting circle suggests protection in general. That it is built around two intersecting crosses with a circle around it embodies Gyfu and Ing, reinforcing the 'magic power' of the spell without particularly skewing its meaning.

I suspect that the notches are more visual reinforcements of the enclosing shape than actual runes, but they may be Niet, causing a binding to hold this "helmet" to the head.

Eohll is the most commonly used rune for protection, often found drawn in all directions, forming either a cross, or around a circle forming a flower like this.

The second simpler protection rune is just that, and combines a circle of four Eohll runes with a Gyfu rune. The omission of Ing and Niet I suspect is a wise choice, avoiding any connotations of the need for endurance, or, how to say it, "extra bells and whistles". I am not entirely convinced that Eohll on it's own isn't more effective.

On the note of exorcism, I'm not a fan. If you genuinely believe that some malign or angry spirit is affecting your life in any way, my favourite exorcism is Sumerian, where an old woman's spirit was tormenting a family. The priests made an effigy of her restored to youth and beauty, gave her a sexy lover, and asked her politely to leave.

Even in the afterlife, blessings are the way.

## Love Runes

Almost a cliché in books on magic, I provide these three love spells, but with lots of notes.

The first (left) spell is a frequenter of books and stalls. It combines the runes in a similar fashion to Aegishjalmir, with this time a very clear Gyfu in the centre. It then reads thus:

Lagu summons the emotions of your intended. Ing brings the curiosity and perhaps fond thoughts, possibly sex.

Feoh is the wealth of belonging and owning.

Mann is binding and marriage.

The next variant (far right) combines.

Lagu summons the emotions of your intended.

Wunna asks that your friendship is strong and fun.

Ing and Birca are the sex runes, male and female.

These love spells are provided in the name of openness and because they do indeed exist. I have now given them, but read on.

They don't work, don't use them, love is not a spiritual contract - it is a spiritual event.

Imagine for a moment that you did a love spell and it genuinely worked. Someone who did not love you suddenly did.

What about all of the reasons that they did not love you? Where are they now? What about the ones that they did love, and the affinities that inspired this?

Imagine that you could cement a love that was dying. Why was it dying?

Add to this the fact that by using a love spell you are foregoing the free will of at least one individual and in this way beginning to scrape against one of the basest forms of slavery. If both parties are willing, then maybe it's alright, but in this instance is it truly needed?

All of us should be desirable and worthwhile in some way without any help. Life isn't always fair or kind, and people make god-awful decisions in love, but the only meaningful tool that you have here is yourself, and if you are in hot pursuit, your interest in that other person.

My final bindrune, in the centre, is a more reasonable request.

Eh represents the friends providing help and comfort. You should also notice that it creates two Lagu runes facing each other to represent the feelings of both parties in harmony. You may notice that I'm allowing a backwards or 'wend' rune. I tend to avoid back-facing or flipped runes as their meaning may change, but in this instance the narrative is obvious enough to ensure control. Note also that Eh already has Lagu in this fashion but that I have emphasised it. Finally, this emphasis creates the rune Gyfu in the process. Gyfu is the rune of gifts, or kisses. This spell is vague enough for you to have to find out which, but I am much more confident of it's succeeding in some way. Your aspiring love may at least become a valuable friend.

It will also be easier to answer if your target has some questions; more a conversation point that heads towards romance than being caught with the magical equivalent of a hanky with chloroform on it.

All cultures have love spells that promise to drag the unfortunate victim of your desire into your possession, yet none of them work.

A single final love spell: Laugh at their jokes, genuinely. Find them interesting, genuinely. Want them to be happy, and enjoy their company. Focus on how great they are, and not how great you are. Make sure that their time with you is happy. Like all the magic in this book that's a really challenging ritual, and not guaranteed to work, but it has hope.

## *Making your own Bindrune*

Here is a really simple two-rune bindrune that I came up with for demonstration purposes. I'm going by the scenario that someone is starting a new job, and basically wants it to go well. Of particular note, they want to get on with everybody, they want to get richer, and they want to enjoy what they do. We could go dead simple, and give them either Feoh for wealth, or Wunna for happiness, and hope that either of these traits would either do, or suggest each other (If they're rich, then hopefully they're either happy enough or competent). However, that seems a little optimistic, so we'll combine them. For the sake of learning, we will do it three ways, and talk about these.

From left to right, the first one here is a definite no for me. We've simply extended the rod of Wunna and branched out Feoh, and it looks a little like a deer's head, which is cute, but we also have created Thorn. Thorn is generally ok on it's own, but it could represent either antagonism or getting stuck here. The second bindrune is probably ok, but Wunna is now a 'wend' or backwards rune. Some mystics see this as having negative connotations, although runes, like hieroglyphs, do not necessarily have to go left to right. I personally just don't like that they are going against each other. Again, this is ok. I'm being a bit fussy here.

The final bindrune, and the one that I'd choose, has overlapped them; we have not made Thorn, and they are both facing the same direction. Finally, you may have noticed that Gyfu has appeared. Gyfu has connotations of gifts and sharing, but also is generally considered good in magic, so whilst not intended this actually makes sense.

## Curses (or no curses)

In my early days, I cursed. It seemed to help me deal with anger to an extent. It also sometimes worked, dramatically. You'll note that some of the Anglo-Saxon runes are unpleasant enough for the purpose, and that was where I headed.

Cursing is sadly rather easy both with and without the Runes. You have probably already guessed that any system that can predict sorrow or misfortune can just as easily invite it. Using methods similar to what has already been described, but with all the negative or reversed runes is no harder than the nice spells.

Don't do it.

Again, there is the issue of free will. What you are unwilling to do with a lock, a gun or a knife should be equally unpalatable in magic; but there is another more selfish reason.

I have mentioned this before; love and hate are muscles. Sometimes we need to go there, but if we choose to overindulge we overdevelop them.

Anger and fear instil both spiritually and chemically a sense of agitation and tenseness needed in our ancient days to keep us alert in the fight. They also tend to create cycles, for anger and fear are things that you can get stuck in. They can become another language, tinting everything that you see.

So forgetting the fact that you are adding pain to an already painful world, selfishly you are hurting yourself by cursing.

If you must tamper with your enemies, bless them. Most wrong deeds are the children of other wrong deeds. Many of the truly unpleasant people that will confront you learned their unpleasant ways from unpleasant lives.

## *The Legible Rune*

*To learn to sing them, Loddfafnir,*
*Will take you a long time,*
*Though helpful they are if you understand them,*
*Useful if you use them,*
*Needful if you need them.*

Figuring out how to symbolise best your purposes and messages with the Runes takes lots of practice, possibly more than a lifetime in some cases. Just writing things down or saying them in a special way also counts.

The spoken word was as important in ancient mystical thought as anything pictorial or symbolic, and still is today.

That might sound obvious, but stressing quite how important it was is worth dwelling on for a moment. Throughout the *Eddas*, emphasis on the value of spoken truths and the damage of lies is tantamount, as is their alleged magical portent. Even the word 'spell' itself is literally derived from the old Germanic word for talking. Similarly, the Christian word 'gospel' literally translates as 'magic utterances'.

Writing down your words gives them a physical presence, and writing them in runes makes them sacred.

Whilst there are numerous historical examples of the Runes being used symbolically, it is often left unmentioned in books like this that the majority of historical finds are in recognisable phonetic words.

Importantly, this includes inscriptions of a mystical nature. Prayers and even possibly complaints to the gods feature on monuments throughout Scandinavia, as well as monuments to both event and friend.

This is far from unique to Norse or Germanic cultures, and one of my favourite examples comes from ancient Egypt, where one of the strongest insults or curses was the removal of names from monuments of the dead, which was believed to diminish or erase the individual.

Messages written in runes will familiarise you with both the passage in question and the Runes themselves, but they also give an easier route for the beginner in symbolic magic. By transcribing your message into runes you also elevate it, in the same way that many people elevate their prayers by lighting a candle, or praying in a church.

As a Pagan you will likely not have a temple, and will have little in the way of holy prayers, songs, and so forth - these you will have to find or make for yourself.

On to the technique.

I feel embarrassed to say this - don't be afraid to make it sound good, including rhyme and alliteration. It may be hard to believe, but the Norse people placed a lot of importance in poetry. The clichéd image of the rhyming wizard is has well-established roots. Like it or not, Walt Disney got this bit right. Norse poetry is often dark and gritty for the modern ear, but in its native tongue it is both beautiful and complex.

Later in this book we will discuss the virtues and pitfalls of the meditative and hypnotic trance, and the structure and feel of any spoken word writing plays a role here. Memorable words are less faltered, if nothing else, but also rendered important. A few of these spoken or written charms survive today, including the Anglo-Saxon "Nine herbs charm", but most were stamped out in medieval times by the church. You will have to make your own.

I would also recommend getting to grips with what a lot of rune practitioners often call 'kennings'. The Norse poems so leaned on by historians and mystics alike are full of them. In my mind, kennings sit somewhere between similes, riddles and a thesaurus. By thinking of an object or person from different subjective angles, you get the benefit of more words to play with as well as a truer sense of its context. This had the dual purpose of fitting the often strict rhythmic, rhyming and alliterative rules of some forms of poetry, as well as engaging both reader and writer in a deeper thought process with regards to said object.

A lot of the understanding that rune practitioners have grafted from the Runes that cannot be directly lifted from texts is gained from this method, where you change the subjective angle to realise the effect of each rune in an array of circumstances.

For a really strong idea of the concept in action, I'd point to the Edda poem, *Alvissmal*, where Thor questions the Dwarf 'All Wise' on an array of subjects. The Dwarf responds with varying descriptive names for each object. This method is more than common in the Edda, for Odin himself has an array of descriptive names which he recites as an introduction in both *Havamal* and *Grimnismal*, but *Alvissmal* exemplifies it:

**Thor:**

*Answer me, Alvis! thou knowest all,*
*Dwarf, of the doom of men:*
*What call they the earth, that lies before all,*
*In each and every world?*

**Alvis:**

*'Earth' to men, 'Field' to the gods it is,*
*'The Ways' is it called by the Wanes;*
*'Ever Green' by the giants, 'The Grower' by elves,*
*'The Moist' by the holy ones high.*

Whatever you write does not need to be in Old Norse, Proto-Germanic or Proto-Indo-European. I enjoy the few phrases I know in Norse. It feels authentic, and from what you have read so far you hopefully understand that this is also valid. It really isn't obligatory though, so don't be afraid of using your native tongue. You can gain insight by digging up another language, but unless you know this language rather well the guesswork that comes along with it might add more confusion than good.

How you write with the Runes, which weren't specifically designed for the English language, is an interesting question. Are you going to spell out 'bridge' with letters (Birca, Rad, Iss, Dag, Gyfu, Eh) or phonemes (Birca, Rad, Iss, Jera)? I have certainly seen both in modern and even old runes. The former is accurate in English spelling, but the latter actually has a hope of being heard purely by speaking the values - neither are entirely accurate.

It is worth giving ourselves the credit that Latin was not developed for the English language either, and is not a particularly good fit. The written English language is already a mess and a miracle of the logical, the borrowed, the improvised and the bizarre.

I personally started with letter equivalent spelling but now head towards just phonemes. This sounds like it matters, but I suspect it doesn't. Certainly runic monuments have heaps of irregularities even when you take dialect into account. The truth is that they are readable, and that is what is important.

I love to see both.

As an important note, many people equate the rune that I call Eohll and pronounce "ay" as in "hay" differently. I know of the two names 'Aquizi', and 'Algiz' being used. The latter 'Algiz' name being much more common in the 21st century by Historians and runic mystics alike. Eohll is also frequently presented as either z as in 'Lozenge', or x as in "I'm a useless letter but the Romans used me, so I must be worthwhile".

In runes, I write 'x', 'ks' as all sane and Turkish people do. I also leave 's' to do 'Z' at the beginnings and ends of words. We currently do this naturally most of the time anyway ('keys' sounds like "z"; 'tasty' sounds like "s").

I would advise writing 'the' with 'Thorn' and 'Eh', as opposed to 'Tyr', 'Hagal' and 'Eh'.

The Anglo-Saxon alphabet is easier for English, as it has a few extra runes for some of the Saxon noises that we use; but note that Ansur becomes Oss, and the Younger Futhark 'H' becomes 'Io'.

It could be argued the Yr is more appropriate for "ee" and Iss is only really meant for the "eye" phoneme.

The Saxons seem to have used Sig and Kaon to make the "sh" noise, such as shoe, and Kaon to make the both the "ch" as in 'choose', and the "ch" as in 'loch'. Please note that this poor fit in both runes and the Latin alphabet is related to why 'loch' in Scotland is 'lake' in England, whilst 'church' in England became 'kirk' in Scotland.

I'd say the other runes were easy enough to let you guess.

It might be worth reading some real inscriptions first. A start to this is provided later in the book.

# Meditation

## *Hypnotic trance or meditative state?*

I have just taught you how to prepare your rune cloth, carve your runes and get out your wizards garb - now I'm going to ask you to put them away.

The following passages in this book deal with ritual, its value and its potency, but also its problems. To explain my mixed appreciation of this, I should clarify what I perceive as the good and bad sides of these practices. This will hopefully show why I keep emphasising the importance of keeping things simple. I do indeed have many books on elaborate ritual on my bookshelf and even recommendations for elaborate costume. Why do I largely shun these?

Step into any religious building and you will be struck by its dramatic levels of décor, pomp and drama. It will probably strike you even before any prayer or ritual has been enacted. Religious places are dramatic. Even the faiths that shun glamour and filigree for more ascetic principles adhere to a hidden law of drama.

Then come the rituals themselves.

Frequently a gathering motivated by faith will involve the following:

- Singing or chanting long passages

- Incense

- Low or high contrast light — for example candles, stained glass, or utter darkness

- Repetitive actions or chants

- Costume - such as religious garments and so-called 'Sunday best'

- 'Follow my leader' style chanting

These processes, conditions and items are important on many levels. Firstly, by getting a community to actively follow simple rules you are connecting them to a common experience; by association with experience or symbol you make learning an accelerated process. Further, you also get yourself into a state where you are generally more receptive. Spiritual exploration is hugely easier in this state — and this is meditation in a nutshell. You are effectively going somewhere else.

These are also the tools of hypnotism, or as it sometimes called, 'suggestion'. It is used by both fraudsters and genuine medical practitioners alike as a method of influence on the mind of their subjects. Hypnosis is a very real phenomenon and was actually discovered, or at least brought into the realms of accepted science, by Dr James Braid who was initially attempting to disprove it.

Why we are able to do this, both to ourselves and to others, is open to debate. I suspect that this weird inner trait helps us to enter states of enhanced concentration for difficult tasks. I also suspect that it helps us avoid awkward situations where our emotions are at odds with our peers. I'm not really qualified to cite either of these theories as particularly worthy of note, though.

However, I do know that the trance state is powerful, and that it can be the route to both truth and untruth.

This is partly why I am careful about being too prescriptive about ritual - and partly why instead of collating and sharing in this book a selection of complex rituals and rules with regards to magic, I am attempting to allow the reader to construct them, or maybe find them independently.

There are also questions of the authenticity of many rituals, and these rituals are frequently either inconvenient or immoral enough to put me off — although right now I want to focus on the trance.

Going back to the trance, I want the reader to be aware of what they are doing. Be very careful about sways. If you insert too much of anything that is likely to be what you get, whether it is true or false. By anything, I mean that something as supposedly neutral as an egg or a tin of beans may end up pulling you by association along a forced path not in line with your intentions - let alone a rune or deity, or even a tree.

Equally, the part of you that feels that something is stupid plays a role. Rituals that make you feel silly are unlikely to get you anything at all. Yes — we all, to varying extents, have a protection mechanism against our tendency towards the hypnotic state. An open mind and a sense of humour is however more than valuable to the mystical explorer, so the trick is to be yourself and expect corresponding results.

To continue my eggy analogy, if you don't like eggs, then eggs probably shouldn't be your first choice, as they may prove to be an obstacle.

Again, the above explains my reluctance to prescribe anything too formulaic, but I now want to give you a sample hypnotic or meditational practice that I use. I feel it highlights the similarities quite well and provides a good backbone to anything you might want to try.

I'm going to call this a blank hypnotic trance. It is 'blank' because it comes with no religious or mystical content. I cannot guarantee that it will work for you but describing it will help explain the process of suggestion anyway.

First, you should find somewhere calm and quiet.

In good weather, outside works well - but you need no distractions. Even irritating blades of grass, dazzling sun or wind can really slow things down.

Get comfortable. Some are able to sit cross-legged, but lying down is the easiest and this option is perfectly fine. For this simple technique comfortable is the rule, and extends throughout this, so at any point feel free to wiggle about and adjust yourself.

Close your eyes and relax. This is more complex than it sounds, as consciously trying to do something and relaxing are initially counter-intuitive. We are used to tensing up for activity or purpose.

Get your breathing into an orderly cycle. Try slow, regular breaths and focus on this. I find it helpful initially to breathe deeply, trying to both pull as much air in, and exhale as much out as I comfortably can to start with. By pushing yourself at the start a little, you can then slip into a regular and relaxing breathing pattern. Also, try and move between using your gut and chest to propel your breathing. Again, you are trying to find the right balance.

When you have the right balance you will feel relaxed, and your breathing should be deep with no stutter or judder.

As an aside, this is really great for you physically - it retunes your relationship with your body, which can become detuned by weird postures and mental states brought about by daily life.

Next, attempt to relax your body. Some of us will already be here automatically, but if not, I go for opposites like this: individually clench the various parts of your body, starting at your toes and moving towards your abdomen; then continue the same thing, starting at your fingers and moving to your chest. So, punctuated by the breath cycles, clench your toes and feet, your ankles and shins, knees and thighs, bum, tummy — and then relax. Clench your hands, lower arms, upper arms, shoulders, torso, full middle and relax again.

You may need to do the same for your facial muscles and eyelids. Scrunch up and then soften.

Again, this is incredibly good for you, but right now we're using it to get you in the right place. You may want to do it again.

Try and maintain your breathing cycle only to the level that it helps. This does not need to go perfectly, mistakes are fine. That it is relaxing is what matters. The tensing process can disrupt a little, but only momentarily. The benefits of added relaxation should be intense quite quickly.

In the meantime, get back to focusing on just the breathing and getting to a perfect rhythm that makes you feel both refreshed and oxygenated. Use the analogy of breathing to bring your mind into relaxation. As you breathe in, you take in new oxygen, which brings refreshment and comfort. As you breathe out, you expel used air. Start doing this with your mind. With each inhale you should try to absorb good feelings, and with each exhale you peaceably let go. Let your mind empty and just breathe. Focus on just breathing.

If distracting or uncomfortable thoughts come into your mind, do not fight them — just let them go. If they don't go away, don't force them out. Try and pacify them with a "not now", or shuffle them to the side with something random.

This stage is the last preliminary stage before you're 'in there' — the waking dream, the trance — but it's also the hardest passage for me to describe.

People move at different speeds here and have different experiences. At this point a hypnotist would be gauging their subject and following their progress with guidance and reassurance, which I cannot do in a book — it's hard enough in person.

This is also the stage where I stop and add what I like to any magical practice. With these things, the results vary, even after considerable practice. Sometimes it all works great and I get roughly what I want, sometimes it isn't.

What we've done here is create a simple starting structure to follow. This method uses breath as the focal point. Many cultures including Norse culture also use melody, recital, dance, endurance, light and drugs to the same effect. We used undeniably factual effects related to regulating your breath to reinforce the validity of the experience, which we then rely on to guide our minds towards first relaxing and then letting go. Our breathing also doubles as a repetitive process similar to the clichéd dangling watch of the psychiatrist or conjurer - a distraction really helps.

Here the departure happens between meditation and hypnosis. If your mind now wanders on its own will, we are in the realms of meditation — but if it is being steered, it is hypnosis.

Everything up to this point is real, safe and helpful. If you try it, I hope you begin to understand the mind-preparing part of ritual. You need to know where you should be in terms of mental state before attempting anything magical. But here is the rub: at this point, suggestion is not just a thing you can add purposefully but something that you may insert by mistake.

In my youth, the more extreme method that I would employ would be to use sensation, a tingling sensation in the extremities to represent complete relaxation. Akin to mild numbness but pleasant, I would suggest that it travelled up the body, until it reached the head, by which time the state of trance was reached.

I would continue this into first a sense of lightness, and then of floating. Once my subject began to see anything in this state, like themselves from above or buildings or clouds, we would know that the sky was no longer the limit, so to speak. A powerful and exciting trance, but rather irresponsible. I was with friends and we were looking for adventure. We got it, we scared the living crap out of each other and had a lot of fun. We learned heaps, but also picked up a lot of nonsense that embarrasses me now, and that I'm frankly unwilling to share.

I hope now that it is evident just how tenuous the border is between bamboozlement and this search for truth. I only practice on myself these days, and it's fairly subdued simply because I discovered long ago quite how wild it can go with hypnosis.

Before trying magic have a good think about what you want from it — and be aware of how easy it is to sway your own results.

Think about what your spiritual subject is in depth: is it overtly positive or negative? Does it leave questions open for your growth, or does it numb you by sending you on your way towards something that you feel that you know?

There is also the risk that if you attempt to enter the mystical state on the wrong tack, you can spiral out of control. This wrong tack can involve you in things that you aren't ready to deal with, either because they are too intense or because you have negative associations with them. Paths can also be wrong simply because they are just wrong; or because your crude understanding of them makes them as good as wrong. Wrong in a trance is not safe.

Actually, I think we could all do ourselves a good turn by knowing the facts about hypnosis, trance and related topics. Placebo, mass hysteria and suggestion play huge roles in our lives. Knowing this relationship helps you to identify and rethink ideas that you have adopted simply because you have been encouraged to do so. It also highlights your own ability to either reach out and truly learn something or completely delude yourself, even by accident. Placebo and suggestion are also frequently a natural phenomenon in human interaction, and useful if understood and used responsibly.

You will need this knowledge to try and get to grips with the Runes. I don't think that any mystical cosmology that I am aware of can confidently be sited as a system whose practices have never been harmful. All of these can become tools of delusion, including religions, science, maths and the Runes. Understanding our capabilities here are tantamount to keeping mysticism safe and honest.

# Runic Meditation

Now let us apply this to runes.

This will be much simpler than the above. To start on a good foot with rune magic is filtering down - not adding.

Your first job is to choose a rune. If this is your first time, I would choose a nice sunny one like Dag or something happy like Wunna.

Start trying to relax. Take a few deep breaths. Don't over do it, your target is deep relaxation and not to pass out. These breaths are merely there to draw a metaphorical line between your magical day and your normal one. You may have a personal ritual already that gets you in the right state, in which case you could add this here at a later date - but for the first time at least I'd recommend nothing fancy. Again, we do not want to colour this.

Then try and picture your chosen rune, as if it was in front of you.

It may help to close your eyes while doing this exercise, but you don't strictly need to.

If you're not thinking particularly runic or relevant thoughts at first don't worry, and don't try to force them out of your mind. Distractions will usually only fade once they've come to their conclusion.

Many tell you to picture your rune on fire or as light, but I'd argue to keep it simple and concentrate on their shapes… Just let the artistic style do what it likes. I usually see them forming from what is called in popular culture the 'stars of the lid': the imagery or substance that forms the noise that you see when your eyes are closed. If you press lightly down on your eyes when they are shut, that is what I'm describing.

Imagine yourself and your rune as emitters, and try to detect the flow of this runic energy. Consider where it wants to go, and where you want to send or take it.

It might help to draw them in front of you with your finger.

Many experienced practitioners in rune magic say them out loud as a way of getting closer to their powers and mysteries. This involves making the sounds of the Runes individually in order to concentrate on them, and access their powers.

For a long time, I personally struggled with this concept because of the many variants of names for the Runes (i.e. Eohll is also known as Eoh, Eoll, Algiz, Aquizi, amongst other names). I do, however, find myself naturally leaning towards doing this, and suspect that most will. This is your choice - it isn't required – so go with what you're comfortable with. When you do this more, you'll know what you need to do.

So, how exactly do you do these runic chants?

On the more pragmatic level of how these chants should be enacted, some would have you shout or sing them. I usually whisper or chant them. In honesty, I'd go with what you are comfortable with. The Runes and the gods are not known to be hard of hearing.

A helpful piece of our spoken heritage to quote here is the part of the folk-tale of *Jack and the Beanstalk* where the giant cries "Fee Fie Fo Fum, I smell the blood of an Englishman". This is often sited as a runic chant inciting the powers of Feoh. Go nuts, have fun.

If you are doing this for spiritual knowledge, let the forces flow over you and any visualisations or emotions move freely in you as you and the rune interact. However, if you are attempting to cast a spell, try to direct this energy towards your chosen subject by either picturing it in your mind or facing it. Visual effigies and souvenirs can be useful too.

After you have finished, be sure to give yourself a bit of time to calm down and smoothly re-integrate with normal life again.

The best way for this is to just to sit down, relax and let your mind do as it will.

That is the simplest form of a runic meditation. If you have just done this for the first time, then well done! Did the earth move for you?

If not, don't worry. Your patience will be rewarded.

You can hopefully imagine that once you feel comfortable with meditation generally, and things like the above visualisations, you can gradually bring all of the additions like charms, magical tools and possibly ritual practices. You are possibly already excited about things to try. That is my intention, but it is good to start simple.

The following sections introduce you to the Northern variant of Paganism that went hand in hand with the Runes, and therein you will find another veritable fountain of imagery and colour to add to this simple start. It is important to me that you do this yourself.

# Runic Pagan Philosophy

## *God Forms*

This is a good point to start looking at the Pagan ideas that went along with the Runes, which may also serve as a muse for your spiritual forays.

The Runes are a powerful tool of magic, healing and personal development within themselves, but they are also intrinsically linked to an ancient belief system. A true understanding of this culture and system is of great benefit.

Even if you question the existence of the gods, they offer us a way to come closer to some of the less understandable forces and energies around us by giving them a human form to relate to.

Before I go any further, I should come clean and mention that my list is incomplete. There is a lot to learn, and for a completely full pantheon of gods both lifetime research and possibly some lucky guesswork would be needed. If the Norse gods truly grab you, this book offers the challenge and not the solution.

Much can be gained by contemplating their subtleties and attempting to understand both the characters of the gods and the corresponding elemental or runic forces they either govern and represent.

People react to this stuff in different ways. Some see it as an interesting set of tales, others see a glimpse of some key truths, and for some of us it's a fully-fledged religion. For those who truly connect with it in a deep way, it is sometimes useful to invoke these ancient deities for insight or to appeal for help in matters that relate to their individual attributes. How seriously you want to take this stuff is really your choice - but knowing it is good.

It must be pointed out that you should be respectful if you wish to consort with the gods. Something more sincere like a prayer is more suitable than the usual cliché of pentagrams, salt and the yelling of demands. These are gods to be respected, not used and abused.

Interestingly – no – importantly - heresy is actually allowed. Many ancient Pagan texts are not wholly respectful of the gods they recall, including Norse texts. People respected the gods and were liable to a bit of grovelling just as they are now, but were also willing to insult the gods, believing that the gods were as likely to shrug it off or take offence as you and I are. One quote that the author Freya Aswyn is both famed for and proud of runs thus: "Never trust a god without a sense of humour."

Expect your behaviour with the gods to go down as well as it would in the pub. However, you are allowed to speak your mind, and ask difficult questions.

Finally, and as an aside, I will mention demons. Norse mythology is crammed with antagonists, some of which are mentioned below. They are not toys either - do not play with them.


## Confusing Gods (Syncretism and Embodiment)


One confusing thing about ancient cultures is that they changed over time, and they mixed with each other.

It is worth taking into account that the Germanic peoples were happy to equate Odin with Mercury for their Wednesdays, and Atilla the Hun is recorded as having Mars's sword (or Odin's, depending on what source you trust).

This also applies to varoius cultures, the Romans being the most striking example.

I feel I need to list a few crazy examples.

Jupiter (Etruscan god) becomes Zeus, but keeps his name.

Tacitus describes the Germans as worshippers of 'Mercury'.

Egyptian goddess Wset borrowed from Greece as 'Isis'.

Turkish sky god (name now lost) adopted and renamed 'Jupiter Dolmenicus'.

In this way, it is quite possible to see that one god could quite easily be another. Norse Mythology has a few odd characteristics, the most notable being three sky gods and the mysterious appearance of new gods.

Many believe that the appearance and battle of the Aesir and the Vanir might represent the meeting of two ancient cultures.

This sounds useful, and it is. Various systems have attempted to merge the gods of all cultures together to create a unified pantheon, particularly in the romantic period of the 19th century. Gnostic groups such as the Rosicrucian order, and later the Golden Dawn, have created neat family trees mapping out these gods and their various incarnations in various cultures.

However, I'd advise a pinch of salt with these systems. Odin certainly isn't the calmer Mercury, Quetzocoatl definitely isn't Celtic Lugh, and Isis so isn't Freya or the Celtic Danann. Reading their tales and rites will show you that very quickly.

So on one hand, understanding many cultures will help. There are parallels. On the other hand, be aware of the mess that Syncretism has already made, and be aware of perfect fits that aren't genuinely perfect.

Another practice worthy of note is the historian's nightmare of, well, embodiment.

One trait of ancient Paganism that now causes a great deal of confusion is how people generally believed that taking on the name of a god, animal or even person would go a long way towards harnessing their traits and abilities.

The closest modern-day analogy comes from Shamanism, which has strong parallels with Northern European Runic culture in my opinion. Shamans describe summoning and taking on the forms of sacred animals to see the world in their light, and perform related spiritual tasks.

We know that the ancients did this, which goes a long way to explain how Celtic characters such as Merlin and Arthur managed to turn up at such improbable times and distances for the age.

This was not seen as deceit, but as a very real phenomenon. Before Christianity it was not in the slightest rare as seen in the names of the Pharaohs of ancient Egypt, who even occasionally altered their titles to show changing allegiance or association with different gods.

A famous example is Tutankhamen, who changed his name from Tutankhaten as a sign of disapproval for his father Ahkenaten's new monotheistic religion. The old name was 'beloved life of Aten', the new name 'beloved life of Amen'.

Again, this comes as a double-edged sword, in that it makes it harder to discern genuine god from average human, but also suggests a form of meditation. I am obviously also not going to try and tell you that it is wise or sane to turn up in your local pub declaring yourself as the living embodiment of an ancient god, but respectfully attempting to step in to their shoes is a valid form of learning.

One final confusing concept: You will note descriptions of the gods largely focus on human forms and attributes, and yet the majority are described as capable of shape shifting. Most Pagans would agree on the premise that these appearances are for us. What the gods would really look like on their days off is utterly open to suggestion. Very little is presented that is not in some way symbolic of their domains. Many people take this motif further, and describe all gods as faces of the one or two gods. I personally do not ascribe to anything as orderly or monotheistic as that, but I do share the belief that when we have spiritual experiences they are simplified down to something that we are capable of appreciating. In short: elephant gods did not appear to Northern Europeans because Northern Europeans would be unlikely to understand elephants.

In truth, the underlying principles and characters in ancient Paganism are globally far more consistent than you may think, with a lot of the core differences being in dressing and not the underlying narrative. Of course, the dangers of finding commonalities where there are none are a risk, as described above, but you'd be amazed at the mass of consensus in ancient thought.

# The Absent or Bad God?

I feel that Paganism, and specifically ancient Paganism, answers a couple of very important questions that I want to share.

All religions face multiple difficult questions, the most common being things along the lines of: "I've been up Olympus and I saw no gods."

Religious books are certainly full of what could be called guesswork, but to be honest if we are to judge an entire philosophy by a selected theory within it, modern science would likely fare no better than any ancient religion. Think Alchemy or Physiognomy if you need examples.

There is the argument that god or the gods are perfectly visible and evident, and that we are just ignorant to it. Consciousness is easy to ignore. Many believe that animals aren't truly sentient, yet I suspect that consciousness spreads all the way down to rocks - whilst I personally couldn't even prove it for apes.

There is also analogy. No astronomer has seen the wolves Skol and Hati chasing the moon and sun, which also don't appear to be drawn by chariots. The underlying idea of hate and fear being the un-doers and destroyers of everything that mankind holds dear still seems to hold true, though. That and the knowledge that without sun and moon, we're in a bad place.

There are, however, harder questions.

One of the most difficult philosophical ideas confronting religious thought today, and throughout history, is that of divine benevolence. Whilst the world around us is loaded with beauty and miracles suggestive of divine intelligence and manufacture, it is also crammed with enough suffering and lack of fairness to suggest that a universally powerful and benevolent god, or even set of gods, is more than lacking.

In other words, if there is an all-powerful and all-knowing god, why is there so much suffering and pain in our lives? Somehow, the apparent invisibility of much that is holy pales into insignificance when this important observation confronts us.

There have been all sorts of suggestions made concerning this, including the idea that our totally benevolent and totally omnipotent god had a 'bad day' and created evil - or that it wanted to test us.

But how can a god of this nature make mistakes? And if a god like this does make mistakes, could it not at least separate the 'good eggs' from the 'bad' on its infinitely wise drawing board, cutting out the gladiator's pit of an imperfect, and for many, unhappy life? This would surely be less cruel.

It has also been suggested that the knocks and bashes of life make us more interesting or valuable — but yet again, couldn't a creator with endless ability just make this all in-built?

The ancient philosophy that the Runes have given us has another angle entirely, and one that I find the most compelling.

According to Old Norse legends, Odin was not the first god, and neither was his grandfather, Buri. The father of the Jotuns (or demons), Ymir, was already present when Buri was licked out of salt by the Great Ox, Audhumla. Interestingly, it does not take long to figure out that they weren't the first either. There is the fire giant Surtr whose flaming sword ignites the ice to create the aforementioned salt as well as Audhumla herself. Then we have the Norns, three maidens, who again were created independently of the gods. It could be said that the universe was already positively crowded before creation in Norse cosmology.

Sadly, there are no hints as to the creation of these entities. Also, note Odin's mother was the Jotun 'Bestla', meaning beast. To give his child, Odin, physical form the proto-god Borr needed a giantess.

Odin was also born neither perfect nor omnipotent - in order to gain supreme knowledge of all things, he had to complete a variety of tasks and sacrifices, one of which included trading in one of his eyes. Journeying to the land of the dead, Odin's trials concluded in his hanging from the tree of life, wounded in a way that would be fatal to mortals.

The completion of Odin's task resulted in his discovery of the Runes, but it also brought about his own sorrow (it is said that he was never truly happy again).

What is interesting here is that these ancient European gods were not seen as all powerful, but as locked in a constant conflict with other forces. Like nearly all religious structures, there was a hierarchy of both gods and Jotuns in their mythos. None of these were ever credited with either being omnipotent or the true creators of the world, however.

The ancient Viking word for the absolute power that reigned over all was one that all modern English speakers are familiar with, albeit stripped of much of its original potency. 'Wyrd' — or 'weird' — traditionally refers to not just the things that we fail to understand, but to the universal power that we are incapable of understanding.

Norse cosmology presents what in modern times we would call the great divine root of all things as a cold mystery, and maybe more importantly as an overwhelming one. This is a sentiment that could be seen as painfully poignant, for we see so much horror brought about by the faiths that so strongly claim to be in cahoots with an all-powerful, benevolent and ultimate truth and god.

Northern Paganism hints at our being not 'cast in the image' of the creator. It doesn't even give us the credit of being its principal concern, for better or for worse. In this philosophy, we are the central concern only of our own gods; the gods of mankind, who are in themselves not invulnerable.

The Runes, however, are meant to be a part of the ancient force that predates even the gods. The gods and giants are shown as using the Runes to gain knowledge and power, and needing to rely on their force for better and for worse. In this way, these strange symbols were perceived as the truest way to 'god', as we like to call it, or the truth. This Runic knowledge comes with the same mix of tickles and stings as our external lives, and the lives of those around us.

There are certain parallels here with other religious beliefs, notably Buddhism, Yogic thought, and to certain extents, Hinduism — but there is a strong departure also, in that the ultimate divine order is not seen in the world of the Runes as either a desirable goal or a force of good. It is instead seen as an unavoidable truth, and if the legends of the old gods are to be taken on trust, it is a truth that can work for or against us — a truth that we might wish to grapple with.

Whilst this may seem strange to us now, many ancient cultures and religions once shared the theme of creators that were not wholly benevolent towards them. For instance, Saturn, the father of all of the Greek gods, tried to suppress and kill all of his sons; likewise Marduk, the King of the Babylonian gods, had to slay his mother Tiamat, in order to ensure the survival of gods and men.

It should also be noted that none of the Runes may accurately be described as either 'good' or 'evil'. Some of them are 'nice' and some of them are 'horrid', but both good and evil can be seen in any of them. Runic ideology, which is more closely linked to nature, has a strong awareness of the fact that the hunt that is evil to the deer, is good to the wolf and the trees.

Having said this, the Runes are full of moral guidance, but guidance that relies not on the pleasure or displeasure of ruling deities, but on the consequences of pleasing and displeasing behaviour in a world where you are neither alone nor unheeded. In other words, by doing 'evil', you are causing bad things by being unreasonable. What you are *not* doing is provoking the wrath of a bearded creator by deviating from his set of rules.

In this way, the Runes offer us a system that allows for a spiritual presence in life. The Runes hint at a consciousness beyond our own mortal lives, but also acknowledge that there is a level to the universe that is, and shall remain, ultimately a stranger to us.

# Odin and Frigga

Odin is the god of the wind, as well as the king of the gods, and embodies three strangely paradoxical ideas.

In early folklore, he often appeared in cold winter nights and at the winter solstice in the form of the "Wild Hunt", where he would rage across the stormy skies looking for people to claim and take their spirits to Valhalla.

Indeed, children in Germany were told that if they weren't good Odin may kidnap them and take them away for a year to learn good manners. Odin also appears in folklore in the role of a darker ancient 'Father Christmas'. In this guise, he would also rain curses upon households that didn't feast in Yule. These are the images of Odin as the strange and awe-inspiring spirit of the night who was not always awaited with glee; the wild god of the dead, and the madness of the storm.

However, he is also the god of knowledge and the Runes.

His most common description is that of a one eyed man with a cloak of grey and blue 'to mirror the sky' and a large hat that droops over one eye.

This eye is missing as he sacrificed it in order to drink from Mimir's well, or the well of memory (called so because the head of the dead god Mimir was placed there to guard it). In this way, he gained the knowledge of all things in the past and the knowledge of how to get the Runes.

This image of Odin, as the hooded god of the wise, was used extensively by J.R.R.Tolkien in his development of the character Gandalf - and indeed many parallels can be drawn between the two figures. He is the old sage and master of mysteries, appearing and disappearing in a flash.

Finally, there is Odin the king.

As the Viking peoples took on a more martial way of life, Odin became more frequently depicted as a king and a warrior. He was

*Facing Page: Odin and Frigga*

also one of the gods called upon by the Vikings to go to war, giving them all the fury of his wild hunt for the battlefield.

The Vikings believed that Odin on-looked all battles, chose the victor and would take those killed in the fray to his home, Valhalla, where they would feast and train for the final conflict at the end of time.

As god of the Runes, Odin is an obvious deity to turn to during any practices involving the Runes, or indeed any magical practices at all. Many respectable rune users include an acknowledgement to Odin as a fundamental part of any rune reading.

He is also a wise choice for issues where wisdom or intelligence are required, as well as communication.

Paradoxically, he is also the god and protector of children and the infirm.

He was often depicted with two companion ravens, named Hugin and Munin, who were said to travel the earth and report back any news. As a result, it is the raven that is sacred to Odin.

The rune Ansur is widely accepted as Odin's rune.

Frigga is Odin's spouse and queen of the goddesses, although she was possibly his daughter as well (the gods seem to have been quite broad-minded about such things). Among other things, Frigga is the goddess of love.

She represents wisdom of an oracular sort; whilst she would rarely tell, she was said to know all things past, present and future. In this way, she symbolises both memory and forgetfulness.

She also embodied the aspects of love and female beauty, and it is said that she would take true lovers to her hall, Fensalir, to live together in a blissful after-life.

Frigga is often breezed over by Odinists as a non-entity, maybe because her legends frequently show her being little more than a naughty wife of sorts.

She steals the gold from Odin's statue and smashes it before Odin can magically use it to proclaim the culprit. After this event, legend tells that Odin left Valhalla - in this time. due to the poor management of his brothers, many evil things were allowed to pass not only into Valhalla but also the world of man.

It should be noted that Frigga is one of the only characters in the pantheon who can trick the king of the gods, and the only one who can upset him enough to make him disappear in a huff for many years.

Frigga is the goddess of the female wisdom and cunning that was able to make or break lives in a time that we now think of as wholly ruled by men. She even wins wars and displaces kings, not with blood, but with intelligence, and is not to be underestimated.

Maybe everyone has just forgotten this.

She is usually described as a beautiful lady wearing white, blue or grey robes and a headdress of heron feathers.

Her sacred animal is the heron and her colours the paler shades of blue, white, and grey, corresponding with her husband. She was also believed to be the patron of dead artists, poets and pious lovers, who would reside with her.

It is said that placing heron feathers under your pillow helps you dream or forget. There is no rune dedicated to her, but Lagu and Birca are good matches.

## Thor and Sif

Thor is the god, amongst other things, of thunder. In picturing him, we are asked to perceive a large, hammer-wielding redhead with a volatile temper.

His red hair symbolises the fire that lightning brings forth and his muscled stature gives us a clue to as its strength. Thor's temper is short, and unpredictable, as thunder is fast, and dramatic.

His task in Asgard is to guard gods and men from the giants, though he was mothered by a giantess; Thunder and hail are meant to be the noise and chips that spark off when he smashes a giant. Thor was probably the most commonly sought after deity on the battlefield. His thunderous presence could be called upon to smite the enemy, as he smote the giants himself. Strangely, though, he is also the god of many peaceful activities.

Thor is the patron god of blacksmiths, farmers, masons, carpenters and all manual labourers, and was more widely worshipped than Odin, the king of the Norse gods.

He was summoned for protection and strength, and his hammer, Mjolnir, is still a popular talisman today.

Nails, anvils and the metal iron were also considered sacred to Thor, and are thus also considered lucky on his count.

The rune Thorn is sacred to him, alongside the colour red and perhaps orange. As guardian of gods and men, he also personifies order and peace where Odin most definitely doesn't.

His sacred animal is the goat, and a goat driven chariot is his transport.

Thor's wife is called Sif.

Sif literally translates as 'Peace' - another hint - but we know little about this goddess, as she is rarely mentioned in surviving legends. What we do know is that she had the most beautiful hair that was compared to the harvest ready cornfields, and that Loki, the wicked god of mischief, once cut it off.

This could suggest agricultural connections or that, as wife of Thor, she represents order.

She is also worthy of note in that if her blonde hair was that exciting to the gods. It seems to suggest that blondes were rare enough among the gods to be notable.

## Njord/Ing and Skadi

Njord is usually referred to as Njord, but is also called Ing, and is represented by the rune of this name.

He is the god of the sea, and represents the abundance and fertility therein. He is also the god of rain, to some extent, and running water.

*Facing Page: Thor and Sif*

In Norse cosmology, the sea is more akin to our ideas of space than it is to our understanding of the sea; it represents the strange worlds both beneath and across. It may even be the case that Vikings believed that the land of the gods or the dead could be reached over sea.

In this way, Njord embodies ideas of male fertility, spirituality and energy.

Njord is one of the Vanir, a separate family of gods that once warred with the Asa, or Odin's family. Their abode is Vanaheim, and Njord's nautical nature may suggest that it was also believed to be across the sea.

After fighting for many years, the Asa and the Vanir decided that they were equally matched, and chose to make peace.

Their first attempts failed and resulted in the slaying of the god Mimir, but eventually they succeeded by a truce that involved swapping hostages, or more kindly described, by adopting members from each other's families. Hoenir had to live with the Vanir, and in his place came Njord, with his infant children Frey and Freya.

Originally, Njord is said to have married his sister who sadly we have no name for. It is this nameless sister that mothered Frey and Freya; but marriage to siblings is prohibited in Asgard, so she had go. He ended up remarrying a giantess named Skadi. After Thor killed her father Thiassi, Skadi stormed over to Valhalla demanding justice, and the gods took pity on her. First, they tried to appease her with a bizarre comedy dance enacted by Loki, who had to tie his testes to a goat. Then, they offered her a husband of her choice, but only on the condition that she chose by the feet. Skadi tried to choose Baldur, but chose Njord largely by accident. Njord had the most beautiful feet - not Baldur.

Their marriage is difficult because they can never agree on where to live. Njord loves the waves and the seagulls, but Skadi loves the snow and the wolves. Their yearly travels from cold

*Facing Page: Njord/Ing and Skadi*

mountain to sunny beach and back is said to echo the cycle of summer and winter.

It is Skadi who chooses the punishment for Loki when the gods finally lose patience with him. Loki insults her in Laukassana, but is also instrumental to Thor's battle with her father.

If you haven't guessed, Skadi is associated with winter and cold mountains. Her name translates as 'Ski', or 'Skate'.

## Frey and Gerdr

Frey, like his sister Freya, is the son of Njord and a Vanir.

He is a god of fertility and usually considered to be the main agricultural deity, but also possibly a god of love and friendship. His name means friend or friendly, and ancient sculptures of him often show his penis erect - so *very* friendly.

Strangely for a god of love, the story of his marriage is complex to say the least. As the tale goes, one day Frey let temptation get the better of him and sat on Odin's chair, Hlidskjalf. This act was not just forbidden, but taboo. Hlidskjalf is a magical chair that boasts a view of the whole world, only for Odin's eye.

From this seat, he saw the giantess Gerdr and immediately fell in love with her. Because of how he found her, he could tell no one, which grieved him terribly. Frey became hopelessly depressed, which eventually troubled the other gods so much that they asked Skirnir, a servant, to find out what was wrong. Skirnir found out everything, and agreed to woo Gerdr for him.

He was sent out on a fine horse bearing great gifts, including Frey's fire sword, to win the heart of Gerdr - but this proved a challenge. Gerdr's father was pleased, but Gerdr herself was less than keen. Stating that she had wealth enough, she refused. I'm afraid that Skirnir changed his tack at this point. He cajoled her with threats of loneliness and even death, before she eventually agreed to marry. Strangely, this marriage of dubious

*Facing Page: Frey and Gerdr*

beginnings survived. However, it is said that the sword that Frey sacrificed for her is the sword that the giant Surtr will eventually use to slay him at Ragnarok.

That the closest equivalent to the god of love both needs and feels comfortable with such a struggle for love could be read in many ways. I'll let the reader come to their own conclusion.

Horses are strongly associated with Frey, and respected characters in Norse Legends have horses dedicated to his honour. Strangely, so are boar. It is a boar named Gullenbursti ('golden bristle') that he is said to ride on.

He also rules Alfheim, the home of the elves, so he could perhaps be seen as king of the elves. I guess that Gerdr did good in the end. Wunna and Jera leap out as Runes connecting with Frey.

## *Freya and Od*

There is some confusion as to whether the identities of Freya and Frigga are not one and the same. In one legend, Freya is unfaithful to her husband, Od. She sleeps with four dwarves to obtain a beautiful magic necklace, and when she is discovered her husband leaves her. No more than this is known about Od, but could this be a mixed up story of Frigga and Odin? Freya is said to wander the earth for some time, in search of her wronged husband, echoing earlier tales of the Sumerian goddess Ishtar and the ancient Egyptian Isis.

Freya is also the master of the Valkyries and appears to be only answerable to Odin, but I feel that she is distinct from Frigga; as distinct from Frigga as sex is from love, and childbirth is to parenting. Where Frigga uses cunning and subtlety, Freya is generally direct. She also frequently ends up being the object of desire in Norse myth. Being considered this eligible by so many again places her firmly outwith the role of Odin's wife.

Freya is one of the more exciting female deities. Where Odin is the god of the Runes, surely Freya is the goddess; her priestesses were as common and indeed highly regarded as shamans and oracles as their male counterparts. Freya represents a form of wisdom, but this wisdom is perhaps the secret

*Facing Page: Freya and Od*

and wild wisdom of nature and the spirit world. The Edda poems attribute 'Sidr', a magic considered specific to women, to Freya. Odin himself is accused of dressing as a woman and using Sidr magic by Loki.

As daughter of Njord, Freya is of Vanir descent, which possibly explains her 'new magic', as well as her rather challenging role as the other really important goddess.

Freya is the patron and representative of women in the throws of agony or ecstasy, and the inner wisdom needed therein. Quite different to Frigga, who deals with the more sedate worries of love or knowledge.

Freya would be called on for help with childbirth, but also for issues of sex, lust and enduring of pain of any sort.

Freya was the patron goddess of cats and allegedly travelled from place to place on a large cat, or a chariot pulled by cats (although they were usually depicted as looking more like Siberian tigers or lynxes). It seems that most female wise-women of the northern tradition were priestesses of the goddess Freya, and it is from her association with cats that the image of the witch's cat is most likely to have come from.

During the plague known as the black death, millions of cats were killed along with their owners due to expected involvement in witchcraft; most ironic, seeing as cats were probably the best defence we had against the rats that spread the disease.

Strangely, while the Freya cult survived Christianity for so much longer than the respective cults of Thor and Odin, our knowledge of Freya and her followers is scant.

The first eight runes of the Futhark are often called 'Freya's eight', which possibly brings up the unlikely connection between Feoh and Freya. I would associate Freya more with Eohll or Birca though.


# Tyr


Tyr was revered as the god of the sky, and many believe that he is connected in origin to the Celtic god Tyrannos. He is also probably the

*Facing Page: Tyr*

closest counterpart in Norse mythology to the Zeus of Greek culture, but in a slightly demoted stance.

He is pictured as an aged warrior wielding a sword. He is one-armed, with a shield worn on the stump of his severed hand.

Tyr lost his arm when the gods were binding Fenris, the wolf god of terror and chaos. Initially the gods tried to integrate Fenris, but he just became too big and wild. Legends say that it will be Fenris who will eventually slay Odin. Fenris allowed the gods to bind him three times as a test of his strength, but on the third time, insisted on a god putting their hand into his mouth as a sign of good faith. None would volunteer but the brave and wise Tyr.

Thus Fenris was tricked. The new rope was magical and unbreakable and Tyr lost his arm in payment for this deceit.

Possibly as a result of this tale, Tyr was seen as the god of Valour, and was summoned to watch over oaths. His symbol, the sword, was sworn upon as a sign of honour.

Tyr also represents wisdom and conviction to one's ideals. Tyr is represented by his own rune, which most believe to depict his sword. In fact, the last eight runes are often referred to as 'Tyr's eight', although this might just be because they begin with this rune.

His connections with honour may also associate him with issues regarding justice and the law.

## Baldur, Nanna and Hodur

The two gods Baldur and Hodur were born twins, but not identical. Baldur was beautiful, lively and cheerful from the day of birth, whereas Hodur was not, and was also discovered to be blind.

When Baldur and Hodur were born, it was said that Odin carved runes on Baldur's teeth; from that day his words were always wise and wonderful. Everywhere he went, all who beheld him would smile.

*Facing Page: Baldur, Nanna and Hodur*

However, due to the cruel tricks of Loki, who was (maybe understandably) resentful of Baldur, he was killed.

The gods always suspected that Baldur would be killed, as Frigga had foretold it, but they got everything to promise that it wouldn't harm him. They literally went to every god, man, woman, every creature, rock, tree that they could think of, and asked all these things to pledge their peace.

To test his vulnerability, they decided to play a game where they lobbed things at him. Because everything had promised not to hurt him, they'd just flop to the floor no matter how hard they were thrown. However, they'd forgotten to ask the mistletoe, which Loki wrought into in to a spear.

He tricked the blind Hodur into throwing the spear, so that he might dodge the blame, and in this way Baldur was killed.

Hodur was executed for his unwitting involvement; which seems cruel beyond the imagination; however Loki's fate was worse. Baldur was, to extents, revived. Hermod, the messenger of the gods, was sent to negotiate his release from the land of the dead, and Hel, the goddess of death, agreed to release him as long as everything in Asgard and on earth wept for him. Even the rocks and trees agreed to weep for Baldur, but Loki, disguised as a giantess, refused. Eventually it is agreed that during summer he can abide with the gods, but in winter he must cheer the dead.

Legend has it that Baldur and Hodur will rule the world when all evil has gone. In this way they both represent innocence and forgiving as forces that one hand are all but completely destroyed frequently but on the other hand can endure where hate fear and vengeance must fall.

Both characters are defined not by their intentions but by their nature, which are in both cases relatively neutral.

Balder represents light, warmth, love and joy, where as Hodur represents darkness, ignorance and neglect (not as traits, but as states of being). Their life and death are symbolic of the yearly life and death of the earth beneath and around us as it moves from season to season. Where Baldur is the warmth and plenty of summer and day, Hodur is the dark and famine of winter and night; likewise they reflect the needs to greet the summer with love and joy, and the winter with understanding and tolerance. Maybe they also represent the summers and winters of our lives.

Baldur's symbol is the mistletoe, and the Odinic people gathered mistletoe in midwinter much in the same way that the ancient druids did - to remind them that the green, the warmth, and the fruits of summer would return. The association of mistletoe with Baldur also connects mistletoe with poetry and art, but please note that it is poisonous.

It is said that Baldur's spilt blood fell down to earth, and that poets and artists are thus arty, because they have mixed with it in some way.

## Bragi and Idun

If you still question the importance of poetry and song among the Norse people, proof is to be found in the fact that there are actually two poet gods (if you don't count Odin). In fact, two poet gods only as long as you don't count the fact that all of the gods and goddesses seem to be able and keen poets.

The ill-fated Baldur, and slightly more fortunate Bragi, are both ascribed with an unusual gift for poetry.

Where Baldur emblemises all that is bright, beautiful and artful, Bragi is specifically the god of bards, skalds and poets. His name is literally derived from 'bragr', the Norse word for poetry.

Like Baldur, Bragi is meant to be wise, a master wordsmith, and a fine singer, although his description is as long bearded, which suggests age over beauty. He is often pictured with a harp or lyre.

In *Laukasanna*, Loki's scolding of Bragi suggests that Bragi is no warrior, and is neither regaled nor honoured thus. Loki basically tells him that he is a coward, and not worthy to enter the debate.

Loki's slandering hints at the uneasy relationship between respect and distaste for the arts that persists to this day.

Bragi is particularly associated with poems that glorify and celebrate people and their lives, and this is partly why his name lives on in the word 'brag'.

In another parallel to Baldur, Bragi is married to a goddess who represents youth. Idun is the goddess that nurtures and provides the

apples that grant the gods ever lasting life. Many believe that the baubles on modern day Christmas trees are derived from homage to this belief.

That Bragi represents an older living poet, whereas Baldur represents a youthful one that must die is worth pondering; the same applies to Idun's association with ripening apples and Nanna's with spring buds.

It is believed that Bragi is Odin's son, but possibly not Frigga's.


## *Loki*


Loki is frequently cited as the trickster god, which is confusing, as Odin is also frequently described as such (even allegedly by himself). Loki maybe more accurately represents deceit and treachery, as well as jealousy and hatred, and is the closest you get to a figure of evil.

However, he can also represents positive things such as laughter and fun.

Although he is a giant, he is adopted as a brother by Odin, and his ability to amuse and appease the gods allows him to be tolerated in Valhalla (until he contrives the murder of Baldur, for which his punishment is to be tied to a rock, where a serpent secretes venom into his eyes until Ragnarok).

Loki is constantly plotting against the gods, whether it is pranks, such as cutting Sif's hair off, building his own armies of evil, or simply getting himself out of trouble.

He beds a giantess called Angurboda (meaning bringer of turmoil) and from this match the monsters Fenris and Iormungard are born, as well as Hel, the ruler of the land the dead.

He also eventually leads the armies of evil in the great final battle against the gods.

His mastery of deceit and trickery has made him a tempting god to evoke in past times. There are legends where he has managed to worm people out of difficulties where the power of Odin, and the might of

*Facing Page: Bragi and Idun*

227

Thor, had been matched, but I doubt that many practitioners would ever use him, except maybe as an example of what to avoid.

As well as trickery, Loki is sometimes the instrument of painful truths, as attested by the Edda poem *Laukasanna*, where he recounts the scandals and misdeeds of many of the gods.

Loki is a sad reminder that evil, in its many forms, seems to have been with us always, and may even be a necessary element for our evolution.

Loki is well represented by the darker elements of the rune Peorth.

## *Hermod*

Hermod is a moderately obscure god, and his most important role in this book is as the god that really might be Mercury. Odin is not Mercury, folks, and this god really makes this clear.

Hermod is Odin's messenger. In the tale of Baldur's death, it is Hermod that is sent to negotiate Baldur's release from 'Hel'.

Interestingly, in other mystical cultures, messenger gods are far more important. They are frequently the gods that are prayed to, like Agni of the Rig Veda, Coyote of Shamanism, or Gabriel in Gnostic thought. These messengers were sought for their help as guides, but also sometimes to lead you to others. I'm not aware of much evidence to that effect in Norse mythology, but feel that a mention is appropriate.

Hermod is the guard of 'Bifrost', the rainbow bridge that leads to Valhalla, and also the ward of the Horn Resounding, which will be sounded at Ragnarok to ready the gods for their final battle.

Maybe that the chief of the gods, Odin, is evidently both willing and able to communicate with all detracts somewhat from the role of Hermod.

Perhaps, if you wish to try actually working with the gods and are unsure as to whom, Hermod is a good first stop.

I would personally align the rune Rad to Hermod.

*Facing Page: Loki*

# Fenris and Iormungard

Fenris and Iormungard are symbols of the destructive forces of the universe, and in the legend of the final battle, or Ragnarok, they are the slayers of Odin and Tyr.

Fenris, with the appearance of a great wolf, is the symbol of chaos as an uncontrollable destructive force.

When the gods found Fenris they took him back to Asgard to try and tame him, but he grew wilder with each day, and with this grew in stature until they feared that they would lose control of him.

He also sired two children, called "Hati" and "Skol", who are the living forms of hate and fear respectively. These two giant wolves are meant to chase the sun and moon constantly, with the hope of swallowing them up and casting us into darkness. This slightly strange explanation for eclipses could be read as a very chilling metaphor.

Iormungard, or the world-serpent, was flung into the sea as soon as the gods found him, but grew and grew until he stretched right around the earth, and was able to put his tail into his mouth.

The Vikings believed that earthquakes were caused by his shifting on the sea floor.

These forces may be acknowledged, but probably shouldn't ever be invoked or summoned.

In the Anglo-Saxon Futhark, Iormungard actually has his own rune, Io, representing that which is beyond your ability or too dangerous.

# Hel

Hel, Loki's other child, rules the land of the 'straw dead' or those who failed to die in battle, and it is from her that we get the word 'Hell'.

However, despite her unpromising name and unpromising start, she cannot truly be pinpointed as bad. NifelHeim, Helheim, or the land of the

*Facing Page: Fenris and Iormungard*

dead, is not described in cheery terms, but it is not a place of fiery pitchforks and torment. It is a cold, dark place of sadness and reflection. In Norse legend, many wise and important people seem to abide here, including not just Balder, but the wise woman from whom Odin seeks council in *Voluspa*.

Warriors did not want to go here, but that could be due to honour; the martial nature of many of the surviving texts from the Viking period may distort this hugely.

Like Coleridge's vision in *The Rhyme of the Ancient Mariner*, she is beautiful from afar, but whilst her top half is of a fair maiden, her legs are blue or dead in appearance.

Generally ancient cultures were worried about the afterlife, suspecting that worries like hunger and discomfort would be measured out as broadly thereafter as they were in life.

That is why people around the world were buried with money, weapons and, in some civilisations, in tombs more akin to mansions.

Wealthy Vikings were frequently buried or burned with their favourite weapons, tools, musical instruments, and regularly with a treasured horse or dog.

Boats feature heavily too.

The image of Valhalla, where only warriors reside in the afterlife, is contradicted frequently, and many texts seem to hint that Valhalla and other great palaces of post-death-rewards also reside in 'Hell', creating an image of something more akin to the elysian fields of Greek legend, or the Duat of Ancient Egypt.

If you wished to talk with the dead, you may come across Hel. Again, respect is probably more relevant than aggression or fear.

I would associate the Yr with Hel.


## Dwarves, Elves, and Jotuns


It feels wrong to explore ancient Northern culture without a general note about dwarves, elves and Jotuns. One of the more entertaining sides to this pantheon is a plethora of 'races' that are seen interacting. To degrees, these feature in the Runes. This gave Tolkien, and the swathes of role-players under his wing, a huge amount to play with.

I do not generally go to them when attempting the mystical, but they definitely make up a large part of the culture (as they seem to do almost globally).

In medieval times, these figures were respected or feared - depending on their virtues or lack thereof.

There are some things to take into account, however. Many of the ancient texts point towards the lines between giant, god, dwarf, elf and man as being rather thin.

Frequently deed, action, or even demeanour, are hinted at as the core differences. Thor insults the dwarf Alviss by comparing his pallor to that of a giant, as an example. Even Fafnir, the Dragon slain by Sigmund in the Volsung Saga, claims that he was once a human, in a what can only be described as a very elaborate speech for any non bipedal beast.

Odin's knowledge and power is earned, traded, and stolen from Jotuns, dwarves, and Vanir alike.

Of particular note are the Jotuns, or 'giants'. Jotuns are often also called 'Thurs', or demon, in Old Norse poetry, and feature as the prime antagonists of the gods.

Firstly and foremost, they are frequently described as big; but most scholars agree not that big. Ymir, the giant that Odin slays and forges into the earth, is evidently quite a large chap, but generally something more earthly is hinted at.

Notably, giants get smaller as time progresses. Ymir and Surtr, the fire giant whose flaming sword spews fire onto ice and triggers the birth of the gods seem to be titanic. Titanic in stature, but also titanic like Saturn - as dark primal forces that the gods must overthrow.

They are usually described as ugly, but again we'll see that this appears to be more a trend than rule, or possibly even question of taste. Frey and Njord both marry Jotuns. Njord is kind of roped into it, but Frey leaps in head-first. I quite like Jonathan Swift's fantastical description of giants. The idea of enormity in itself giving you a close up view that's not flattering, but evidently the population of Jotuns was not without its stunners.

Whatever these Jotuns looked like, legend makes it clear that they are quite capable of both intercourse and childbearing with the gods. Odin and Thor have Jotun mothers, and offhand it is quite hard to think of a god or goddess who hasn't slept with either a Jotun, a dwarf, a human, or even in Loki's case, a horse.

They are generally meant to live in Jotunheim ('Jotun Home'), which is pictured as a cold mountainous dark place.

They are also perceived frequently as evenly matched. In the Edda's description of the end of the world, 'Ragnarok', Jotuns play a significant role in the demise of the gods.

The similarity between the idea of Jotuns and the ancient Greek and Sumerian old gods should be noted here as important. There is a common theme of our creators or their forebears being adversarial in nature. I personally am more comfortable with this than I am with the also-common idea that everything was great and either we, or the gods, wrecked it. It also goes a long way to explain the existence of suffering and sorrow in a world ruled by gods.

Folklore is also abound with encounters, but these nearly always end badly.

Then there are dwarves and elves.

According to legend, when Odin slew Ymir and rolled him into the lump that we now call earth, he went away to plan what creatures he would place there.

When he came back he discovered that beings already lived there, a common theme in Norse myth, where even the gods are preceded. Unwilling to kill them, but also unwilling to hamper his plans, he decided to separate out the good and the bad among them, and place them elsewhere. The nicer ones he made elves and gave them Alfheim as a home. The others became dwarves or dark elves, and he gave them Svartalfheim ('Dark Elf Home').

Elves are sacred to the god Frey, who was given Alfheim as a 'tooth gift', presumably when he was teething. They are meant to be wise, beautiful, and excellent with words, song, and dance.

Light elves feature minimally in the Eddas, but folklore has them as useful friends and dangerous enemies like the more familiar Celtic fairies or Scottish brownies. Often places of intense natural beauty or spiritual harmony would be considered as property of dwarves or elves, where offerings could be left to please them, or wanton fouling might offend them.

Dwarves, on the other hand, are meant to be excellent craftsmen and are drafted to create, among other things, weapons for the gods - like Thor's iconic hammer, Mjolnir, and Odin's spear as well as the chains that bind Fenris and other items.

They are meant to live underground in mines, where they find precious things.

Usually their role in the sagas is of traders, but almost invariably they are considered as beneath the gods. Thor's disgust at the idea of his daughter marrying Alviss, and his trickery, show these attitudes well. However, the fact that Alviss is indeed so wise, and does at least fancy his chances, again hints at them not being so utterly different at the core.

Remember that Freya sleeps with four dwarves to get Brisingamen, a necklace of unrivalled beauty.

The actual balance of good and evil between the elves and the dwarves is fairly ambiguous, as is their status.

On ground level, among mortals, the folklore is even more muddled. Dwarves are generally perceived of as ugly, but this is not a rule, and both parties are capable of good or ill in equal measure.

Interestingly, dwarves and elves evidently are far more universally recognisable across the globe than any gods. Their traits are remarkably similar from culture to culture, and in this way you already know more than you think.

Strangely, this may be related to fact. The morally abhorrent act of getting smaller people, and even children, to do certain seemingly unconnected tasks (including jewellery, fine craftsmanship, and mining) stretches back to before history, and sadly right up to the present day. Ancient Egyptian jewellers employed children for fine detail made by tiny hands and eyes that leant towards myopia, or close sightedness. I am afraid that modern clothes factories in some countries still do. Ditto with the ability to squeeze into tight places – a practice sadly alive into 19th century Europe with chimney sweeps, and the present day in lithium mines in Africa.

Obviously, I prefer the idea of the elves that dance under the moonlight and sometimes befriend mortals to exchange knowledge and treasure. The Scottish legend of Thomas the Rhymer hints at travel to distant beautiful lands, and the learning of ancient poetry. All of this appeals to me, but I personally lean towards animals, trees, or the god themselves when I reach out.

# Animal Totems

Animals are used in all cultures as a means to understanding the spirit world, and if we are truly to understand the Runes as a system, we are going to have to look closely to the world that they reflect.

Many folk tales and superstitions are still around today, to remind us of how important the animal kingdom was to our ancient predecessors.

Certain animals we admire, and ever since we arrived on earth we have been using a host of them either as providers, messengers, or companions.

There are also animals that we fear and respect - or at least there were until we started building cities.

Either in effigies or in the flesh, animals can be used to connect with their specific energies and extract a greater knowledge of the world around us, and thus the Runes.

While it is impossible to list all of these sacred animal images in one volume, let alone one chapter, here are just a few of the associations that the ancient Northern people held with animals - many of which are still regarded seriously today.

I've only included animals that either are treated very differently in Norse culture or described in particular depth. I should also add that the ideas put forward here are to suffice as an introduction to how animal understanding relates to the systems and beliefs of the Runes and the gods, and should by no means be considered a complete explanation.

# Important notes on sacrifice

Right from the start, I should declare that I neither sacrifice animals nor condone it, but I feel that the subject needs covering and here strikes me as the best place to do so.

We are fairly sure that sacrifice happened, but not sure how and why. I personally debate the validity of quite a lot of it, as well as question the rather sweeping ethical debate that tars our ancestors so generously with insults.

Even in language, it is clear that sacrifice occurred in early Northern communities. For instance, the Viking word 'blot' for meeting, and the Saxon word 'blessing' are both descended from words that are cognate with blood. There is also a fairly detailed description of a human sacrifice in the form of Ibn Fadlan's account of a Viking boat burial in what is now Russia.

Now for some mind games. While it sounds fairly abhorrent, this account certainly makes it clear that consent was involved, and that the victim evidently believed that they were quite literally heading off to a better place with the dead man that was to be burned. They actually describe seeing this place as part of the ritual.

Usually sacrifices ran thus, with the victims being elevated to holiness, and the perpetrators of these despicable acts, at least on the surface, believing that these sacrifices were actually being honoured in their own right. This is partly why I debate the validity of many 'sacrifices'. As an example, if you've just sent someone to the gods, you're probably not going to send criminals - and you're probably not going to shamefully hide the evidence head down in a ditch.

This lengthy discussion is not because I do not find this abhorrent, but because I find the snorting at sacrifice by many who are willing to sacrifice animals to their gut somewhat unfair.

Personally, I do not see it as anyone's place to choose an animal, or indeed human, and either force or coerce them into a gift of death - but the turkey at the Christmas table seems hardly more enlightened in its conclusion, if I am to be honest.

All of this said, I again stress that animal sacrifice is to me out of the question. I neither practice nor condone it.

If you feel the need to bless with offerings, I happen to know that the gods and the Runes are huge fans of fine wine, nice sandwiches, and plenty of other much more humane offerings. It truly is the thought that counts, and even that is on the basis that what is being measured is your willingness to give. The staple in most modern practices is incense, which smells great too. In fact, if you really want to make Odin or Thors day - why not feed a raven or a goat?

Good paganism rejoices in life, here and now.

## *Oxen*

It may seem strange for people in modern western culture to think of the cow as a particularly spiritual animal, and place it in front of new age favourites such as the wolf, the cat, or the stag.

Likewise, it may be hard to pick them out as a creature we either relate or aspire to, but the first two runes of the Futhark, Feoh and Ur, depict various sides of the ox. Interestingly, the letter 'A' of the Greek and Roman alphabets also depict the cow. This shows us that cows were vitally important to the ancient peoples of Europe.

Cows were highly esteemed. It was a large cow, Audhumla, who was said to have triggered the creation of the universe.

The milk that they provide is still used today as a major part of our diets, and the diet of our young. The cow was seen as a symbol of not just wealth, but the nurturing motherly nature of the world.

Even this is probably a huge demotion from their original status, being widely prevalent in most religions and even the first cave paintings.

Likewise, the second rune, Ur, refers to the Auroch. The Auroch was the ancestor of the modern cow, but also a strong analogue in almost every way to the American buffalo. They were seen as symbols of raw strength and bravery.

This combination of strength and nurturing energies is utilized all over the world by the hanging of the heads of oxen in houses, or on entrances as protection from evil powers.

This elevated homage to oxen is not restricted to Norse culture. The goddess of beauty in Ancient Egypt, Hathor, was the patron of cows, as was the Sumerian queen goddess Ishtar. The fates of Gilgamesh and Enkidu are finally sealed when they slay the bull of heaven, offending Ishtar in the Epic of Gilgamesh, which currently is the oldest written story known on earth.

If you want to come to terms with any religion, it's probably worth rethinking the cow.

## Cats

Cats were sacred to Freya; the goddess connected with female magic, sex, intuition and childbirth. They were thus revered and persecuted alike as our society's attitude to the old ways changed.

As representatives of the goddess Freya, cats were seen as protectors, as well as messengers to the spirit world until their connections with her cult made them perceived by the Christians as symbols of devil worship. Ironically in the time of the Bubonic Plague or 'Black Death', which should have been their finest hour, they were hunted and killed en masse, along with their owners.

Our best natural defence against the plague rats was betrayed by the ignorance of man.

So cats are powerful allies for all those concerned with the ways of magic; as guides, protectors, spirit contacts and of course, companions.

# Dogs and Foxes

Viking burials and common folklore around Northern Europe testify hugely to both love and admiration of dogs, but strangely I have found no association with any god, goddess, or rune. Stranger still, this is echoed elsewhere. We also know that dogs were loved in Ancient Egypt, to the extent that they were given human names in the home, where the humble cat was just 'miw' or 'cat' but again no dog god.

Anubis is not a dog, as we will see.

Similarly, foxes are largely absent in runic lore, even though they are abundant in folklore - but this is almost unique in that most cultures place huge weight on either foxes or their equivalents. Foxes, jackals, and coyotes feature strongly as guides, particularly with relation to the spirit world. Good examples being the jackal god Anubis in ancient Egypt and Old Man Coyote of American Shamanism, who are both pivotal deities in their respective cultures. They are both key providers of wisdom through guidance and example alike.

Then there is cunning, and frequently the championing of the underdog. The fox is frequently chosen as the symbols of the suppressed, and their ability to win over their privileged oppressors.

This association with the underdog may explain their absence.

One of the reasons why Norse culture survived, even in fragments, is because the aristocratic classes were not entirely willing to let go. What we have written down in the Eddas spent much of its life in the dusty libraries of kings. A well preserved yet incomplete record thus biased towards the thoughts of said kings. This thought is worth dwelling upon.

# Wolves

The absence of dogs and foxes may be compensated by the almost pivotal roles of wolves in Norse mythology.

Wolves have the same mixed emotional tones now as they did for the ancient northern Europeans. Odin is occasionally depicted with wolf companions as well has his raven friends. These wolves are called Geri and Freki ('ravenous' and 'greedy'). They seem to be hunters of the slain in the style of the wild hunt, as opposed to guides - like his ravens.

There are also some really bad wolves in Norse mythology. The wolf Fenris, who embodies chaos, comes to mind. Legend has it that he will be the one that eventually kills Odin, and his children aren't much better. Skol and Hati are quite literally fear and hate embodied as huge wolves. It was believed that together they chase sun and moon, sometimes briefly catching them and causing eclipses and strife. It was also believed that one day they would finally manage to swallow the sun and moon, plummeting the world into darkness and signalling the end of times.

'Rolf','Dolf', and 'Ulf' are common in wolf related Norse names, either alone or combined as in 'Ulfric', 'Rudolf', etc. That they were honoured to some extent is without question, but with more than a pinch of fear.

So wolves are acknowledged, but with caution. They are possible bringers of wisdom, but possible deadly foes.

It is worth noting that European wolves are somewhat larger and more threatening than the now more commonly known American wolf.


## *Ravens*


Ravens have always been considered as divine birds by the peoples of Northern Europe, and the raven still features on many family crests as well as the current German government flag.

Their habit of frequenting recently used battle sites to scavenge for human flesh has likely given them their association with Odin, but their associations with both nobility and magic may run deeper, and are still evident today.

Ravens were sacred to Odin, and were seen as guides to all seers - Odin was said to have been aided by two ravens named Hugin and Munin (respectively meaning 'thought' and 'memory').

Popular superstition in Britain has it that houses populated by ravens are blessed, and when they leave a place, it is a bad omen. There are actually cages and carers for the ravens in the tower of London, because their leaving would be seen as an omen that Britain would be defeated as a nation.

Many magicians and witches were also believed to be able to turn into ravens or crows, in order to travel great distances and view the world.

Ravens are painfully clever, so this huge elevation in magic is not surprising.

## Swans

Valkyries, the maidens who collect the warriors from the battlefield to Odin's will, are meant to be able to shape shift into swans. One of the most famous Norse tales, that of Weyland or Volund the Smith, actually describes young men catching them without their swan robes and keeping them as brides - yet there is much more to it.

Norse, Saxon and other European folklore and legend are literally crammed with these elegant and yet feisty birds.

Shape shifting is a common theme, attested most blatantly in the legend now most famously known as Tchaikovsky's ballet, *Swan Lake*.

It may be the full frontal arrogance of swans that clinched them in the Northern mind as more than meets the eye. It may be their relation to both sky and water, and it may just be their good looks.

Their association with Valkyries places swans firmly in the patronage of the goddess Freyja. I wonder how they get on with the cats.

I associate swans with the rune Lagu. Don't let their beautiful and orderly forms hide their strong ties with the equally beautiful but raw and chaotic side of nature.

I am one of the few that suspects that swans are, if anything, somewhat underestimated. Investigate them.


## *Herons*


Of all the elegant and mysterious birds that could hold the patronage of the goddess of love, it is the wonderful, but somewhat gangly, heron that holds this honour in Norse culture.

This struck me as odd on first introduction, but further examination shows this to be a common motif. Isis, the ancient Egyptian goddess of love, is connected strongly to the Ibis - another large wading bird. The Lithuanian nursery rhyme *Gandrai Gandrai Gagaga* associates the stork with witches. The stork, of course, is also accredited with dropping off babies by particularly prudish and dishonest parents.

So, there really does appear to be a strong connection between wader birds and the goddess of love or motherhood in the ancient mind.

Wader birds are dramatically the masters of land, sea, and air, making them the masters of two great mysteries to man. Frigga is definitely the mistress amongst the gods who is said to hold the mysteries that perhaps even Odin is unaware of. They also have a habit of pulling their sustenance both from the impenetrable deep and the supposedly empty sand; this may connect them with fertility.

Finally we have the fact that whilst the heron in itself does not always scream elegance their feathers are particularly dramatic and beautiful, and suited for clothing and decoration.

Maybe now we come close to the roots of this mystery.

# Boars

The boar, being sacred to Frey, was associated with fertility and virility.

Boar were important in many cultures for their noted ferocity and bravery, which somehow contradicts their association with a generally peaceable god.

In medieval times, knights needed bulges on their lances to hunt for boar, as they were known to continue their charge once impaled, right up to the hands of their foes. If you meet a boar in the wild and they are behaving aggressively, they are one of the few animals that you are unlikely to win over with a brave stance.

# Horses

Part of the fun of horses here is that they help us date a lot of what we now recognise to be Northern or runic culture, to at least after the arrival of horse riding in Europe. Horse riding is thought to have spread from the steppes, and only reached Europe and Africa comparatively late compared with the rest of the animals here. Writing is older than riding in many parts of the world, and many ancient writing systems don't mention it. They were probably introduced via Mongolian tribes - again, a fascinating connection.

However, the horse features in runic culture and religion dramatically.

The ancient Europeans saw horses as messengers to the gods, as well as a mode of travel. Soothsayers of the Northern traditions watched their sometimes-erratic behaviour, similarly to the way of original American soothsayers, and would make life-changing decisions based upon what they saw.

Horses draw the sun and moon across the sky, and one of the most exciting archaeological finds was a large prehistoric bronze horse and cart carrying a sun found in Norway.

Horses also have their own dedicated rune, Eh, connecting them with concepts of friendship and aid.

Odin has an eight-legged horse, named Sleiphnir, that can fly and features strongly in many legends - but horses seem most commonly associated with or dedicated to Frey.

## Deer/Elk

As well as being the elusive roamers of the woods and providing a valuable additive to our diets, these magestic creatures have inspired mystics and shamans alike, notably by virtue of two unusual traits.

Firstly and most obviously, their horns were regarded as an incredible statement of strength. Many European images of gods are given the antlers off a deer or elk as symbols of their natural divinity.

Secondly, and maybe less apparently, their bladders also caught the imagination of our ancestors.

Members of the deer family are both attracted and immune to the hallucinatory mushroom, Fly Agaric, which is the red and white spotted mushroom that frequents children's books and fairy tales.

The Shamans of Lapland still use these mushrooms to attract the deer, as the creatures seem to actively seek out this strange food. When they eat these mushrooms, they start behaving quite erratically.

In fact, it is the habit of reindeer to leap exaggeratedly whilst under the influence of Fly Agaric that has given them the place of honour in front of Father Christmas's sleigh - but there are yet more surprises.

The kidneys of the reindeer actually filter out the more dangerous chemicals, leaving only the moderately dangerous and strongly hallucinogenic ones in their urine, which Shamans would then drink.

The image of the deer can thus be used either as a symbol of transport into other realms, or an image of strength and majesty, and a declaration of personal belief. Combine this with the fact that most species of deer are forest dwellers, and it is no surprise that mystical portent abounds.

Some believe that the rune Eohl represents the elk, and certainly Celtic legend features deer as guides to woodland secrets.

## *Goats*

Goats are associated with Thor. This may associate goats ironically with strength and protection, but that is guesswork.

The Romano-Turkish thunder-wielding goat drawn sky god, Jupiter Dolmenicus, has simply too many parallels not to hint at Thor and his goats being an older tradition than you might think.

Notably, in most religions goats are perceived of as far more benevolent than they are in modern cultures; as feisty but generally peaceable and useful beings.

Even in Christianity, association between goats and the devil only really took hold in the Dark Ages. It does not feature directly in the bible. Goats are sacrificed both directly to god and as scapegoats where people place their sins on the goats and abandoned them, but no direct association is made with the devil.

I personally know little about goats, but they do not appear to be malevolent, and they do appear to like brown bread. More investigation is required.

# Afterthoughts

## *Is this part of a religion, and does it have a name?*

Yes and no.

The Runes do not need to be religious, but they certainly point that way for many - including to some degree, myself.

While there are rune practitioners who are openly Christian, such as the prolific Ralph Blum, generally rune users feel the need to share it are Pagan; and generally their Paganism is with reference to the Norse gods.

The four names I know of that are usually specific to runic paganism are 'Heathen', 'Odinism', 'Asatru', and 'Northern Tradition', and they all have slightly different connotations.

Throughout the writing of this book, and indeed throughout my life, I have been unsure as to which of these titles I am more comfortable with. If pushed to make a decision and unable to evade the question, and only then, I will call myself an Odinist. I will explain why this is so, as well as why it is uncomfortable.

Like many descriptive names of ethnic or cultural groups, the terms 'heathen' and 'pagan' were originally intended as insults. Where 'pagan' means 'country folk', 'heathen' means 'dweller of the heath'; both being used by early Christians to refer to the uneducated peasantry.

Many rune practitioners use the word 'heathen'. The differences and the preferred choices probably lie with the earthier side of Paganism appealing to Wiccans, and the wilder side to rune users.

Heathenism is also more suggestive of a Shamanistic wisdom as opposed to a more classical pantheon- based religious system — but that is through vagueness, as opposed to something stated.

I feel that the terms 'heathen' and 'pagan' unfairly represent not just myself, but many global cultures. I do not want to stand beside a Hindu priest or original American shaman and state that we are collectively the uneducated, which is the underlying theme of both words.

This insults what we share, as much as it insults what we don't.

Within their etymological roots, these terms also impose a rural theme to both the culture and people described - and while I love nature, I will always be drawn to the city as many 'pagans' were before Christianity.

'Odinism' and 'Asatru' are both attempts at a more formal description of a religion as defined by the set of beliefs and accompanying pantheon of gods. Obviously, rune users who see the mythology as an interesting selection of useful codswallop would avoid these names. Asatru literally means, 'true to the Asa'. Odinism suggests an adherence or belief specifically in Odin. In my limited experience that description isn't unfair, in that while most practitioners are clear and knowledgeable about the rather complex pantheon that is the Asa, I am yet to meet a 'Freya-ist' or a 'Tyr-ist'. In modern terms, those who go for the gods at all could maybe be best described as belonging to a cult of Odin, if anything.

The term 'Asatru' feels authentic, but has been co-opted by some fairly racist groups, so I'm not wild on it. Odinism tends to be the chosen phrase of those who are openly against racism, but not always, in my limited experience.

However, 'Odinist' describes me — not as a follower of a religion that I would have the world adhere to, but of Odinism as a cult in the true sense of the word. As a comparison, a Shivanista is someone who is a follower of Shiva, but who does not at the same time abandon the entirety of Hinduism. One of the fun things about the tales that survive is that they leave plenty of doubt within their cosmological structure, as I feel that all good philosophical and religious doctrines should. My personal path involves many cultures, but above all Odin. This does not mean to imply that I feel Odin is superior to all other gods — but that he is the one I connect to personally. I also invite you to note that the Odin I connect to is not the warrior king Odin, but the wild sage Odin; the Odin who wanders the earth teaching and testing his peers, the Odin that undergoes complex ritual and ordeal for the truth and the Odin that even gets caught dressing up as a lady and doing 'woman magic'. I write of the Odin that will do just about anything for knowledge.

In this book I have used the term 'Northern tradition'. Again, I am not comfortable with all the associations this term might come with. The term implies, for example, a geographic location that likely matches only a tiny percentage of the content — but it does one good thing. It places the feet of the heathen, the savage, superstition, and magic firmly on wet ground and under cloudy skies.

Modern western culture still sees non-monotheism as a burden and a privilege only for non-Europeans.

A good look at our own pasts, as well as glimpses into other cultures, shows the Runes and the gods to be part of a huge beautiful world-scoping heritage that should be acknowledged. It also goes some way to stress that the religion is not merely 'Viking' just because the best records survived with these individuals. A broader region and culture of Northern Eurasia is described in runic lore —not just that of the warrior classes of Scandinavia.

## *Is there a moral code?*

This is important to me. Forgive the rant.

Some modern Rune practitioners will sell you a loosely organised and frankly quite embarrassing set of moral codes as part of the Northern tradition, usually pointing in the direction of some kind of martial ancestor-worshipping moral code. I want to argue against this.

Firstly, talk of ancestors is problematic. By adopting Paganism, you are likely upsetting your parents at least, and your less direct ancestors may have burned you at the stake. You are definitely not honouring your recent ancestors by being a Pagan, or indeed using the Runes.

Secondly, your ancestors most definitely did not honour theirs. They abandoned their culture, defaced their own monuments, robbed their own graves, and lied through their teeth about their ancestors. When archaeology matches history, we get excited because it is quite rare.

So please take it with a pinch of salt when people mention honouring ancestors. They honour the ancestors that they like the sound of.

Next, I struggle with the tenet-based structure of morality that people seem to feel they need to have with regards to their religion. Ideas that regularly appear in this context include honour, valour and the solemnity of oaths.

Certainly, the Viking sagas are crammed with this — but read again. Even these same texts hint at the sharp edge that meets both god and man who seek only justice, or vengeance. Honour is frequently abused by both villain and hero alike as mere tools for their desires, just as it so frequently fronts greed and spite today. The heroes of the Viking sagas, whatever they exemplify, reliably come to grim endings — and this occurs often enough for the word 'saga' to be adopted into the English language as a term for long sequences of awful events.

Most of the truly successful exploits of the gods are victories of wit or negotiation — with battle or revenge nearly always ending in misery for all.

As a note, a gift of a sword or even a ring from the gods usually results in the annihilation on an entire bloodline or two. Take that as you wish.

Being more specific, the Havamal claims to be the advice of Odin, but it is earthy advice, offering guidance on how to survive and prosper as opposed to attaining spiritual peace. While all of it is worthy of note, some advice comes across as fairly dark and sarcastic. Of all Norse texts, I definitely would not choose it as my moral grounding rod.

What should be clear about the Eddic stories of the gods is the lack of sanctity for any values, other than life, and what is the perceived as the common good. The Gods personify both truth and lie, and most of the accompanying legends contain riddles and half-truths as pivotal plot handles. Fidelity both in love and war are called for, but are as just as often broken. Any rule or virtue cited in *The Elder Edda* that I can think of is duly broken by the gods.

Considering this as an overall theme, I find myself strangely okay with that. Rules in themselves can only imply good behaviour, which to me is more of an intelligence test than a set of rigid tenets. For me, it is difficult to place honour anywhere other than with pride, and by association with a hypocritical kind of smugness. Behave well for others, and not your name or your image.

But yes, there is a moral code - it is the Runes themselves.

Feoh - to be truly wealthy in life or in love, you will need to give up a lot. The owners of many things are also to be owned.

Ur - status is real, understand that sometimes you must blow your own trumpet or smile sweetly when others blow theirs.

Thorn - things and people can get in your way, but remember that they have their place and purpose too.

Ansur - listen and talk honestly, true wisdom requires both.

And so on.

The Runes paint a picture as full of the things that we'd rather avoid as it is with the delights of existence. They suggested a tempered approach to troubles and blessings alike, and they suggest to me, ironically, a merciful approach to much of what we condemn in ourselves and in others.

## *What Next — Practice*

By now, you will have a grasp of the Runes and their underlying culture.

Most importantly, you have the meanings of the Runes, and it is this cosmological structure that you need to understand in order to attempt runic magic.

The myth and legend herein should also help, by adding a little context. As a rune user your job is to describe the entire world within the remits of twenty-four symbols. An understanding of the beliefs of the people that used them will help you do this.

Fortune telling has hopefully been dealt with in a fairly meaningful way. What you should now have, combined with a little common sense on your part, is enough to do consultations for yourself and for those around you.

Wisely used, you now have a second ear to the world — a second opinion that should provide insight into situations that would have been hard to gather on your own. This should make the Runes both entertaining and informative. Whether this makes you a useful conversationalist or a prophet of future events comes down to your skill.

I want to stress again, that playing and improvising are important as techniques within their own right. The methods that I've introduced are not cast-in-stone sole solutions, but an introduction to the ethos. Go wild!

Magic spells and meditation? Well, this is harder.

In writing this book, I struggled between the desire to give you a unique and elaborate system and being authentic to a working system that was used by ancient runic practitioners. What I have been able to present is that stuff is out there, but a lot is omitted or skimmed over because it is not reliably proven authentic or well preserved enough for us to truly understand it.

Where I hope to have excelled is in highlighting some of the known mechanisms at work, as well as their potential benefits and pitfalls. I am hoping that it is fairly clear that each person has slightly different needs if they wish to progress on this path. If you don't like a magical practice, it probably won't work for you. Your own mind is both your most powerful tool and your most difficult hurdle.

It takes patience, skill and factors obtuse enough to call luck before very much can be guaranteed in terms of reward. I have also hinted at the fact that actually knowing what you really want, and what is allowed, are also fairly important factors. If you wish to exert your psychic will on the world around you, try to have a good idea of your method and your goal, as well as their potential consequences. Discarding their actual potency, the Runes help you focus on what your objectives really are, as well as providing simple visual prompts and tools to exercise your focus. In this way twenty-four truths is more than enough to begin your journey, and with regards to actual practice, improvisation is likely to be one of your best friends.

Further exercises regarding the Runes go in two directions; research and intuition.

I've already mentioned this in reading the Runes, but what have I missed? Any individual is only capable of a limited world-view. What of your experiences are you not finding in someone else's description of the Runes? Your whole life should be in there, as well as that of all of your peers.

What feels unbalanced, and why? The process of threading real life experience into the Runes is the beginning of understanding them.

Note your confusions; they might get an explanation later on.

Possibly most importantly, enjoy it. A whole world of concepts and characters awaits you; a world that out-spans any film or novel and a world that defies your expectations

## *What Next — Reading*

Don't trust me - get more books.

Concerning specifically rune books, Nigel Pennick's books contain a plethora of interesting fact and theory. His books tend to lean towards being longer and harder to read due to their academic nature, but as references they are as valuable as they are fascinating. Of particular note is the range of folk tradition and Saxon culture, which permeates life, language and culture in most of Northern Europe.

I also recommend Freya Aswynn, who has an in depth knowledge of the Norse and Frisian cultural side to the Runes, as well as a strong grounding in more conventional Magick. Again, her books are large, but generally they are easier to read, entertaining, and informative.

For easier rune books, and possibly a gentler feel, Ralph Blum and Tony Willis are recommended. Designed as beginner's books like this book, they might prove useful backup where you question the contents herein.

Then there is your own research.

Read the *Elder Edda*, you won't regret it. It is beautifully written, at once both mysterious and full-frontal. Listen to dragons gasp their last words, and watch the gods forge their destiny with laughter, sweat and tears. You can smell their breath in the text.

Jackson Crawford strikes me as a trustworthy guide to the historical backdrop of the Runes and mythology, and has online videos as well as books on the *Edda*.

Then there are other cultures to consider. The dry writing style of many ancient Egyptian texts is made up for by its mixture of humorous and mystifying symbolism and imagery. Assyrian texts, like the *Eddas*, are abound with renditions of characters so living and feeling that you can hear their footsteps. The Shamanic tales and teachings of the Original Americans and Finnish Suami are particularly poignant when you are trying to get to grips with the more animally side to the Runes (which have a particularly large animally side), as well as being both charming and relatable. Then there is Hinduism, which has so much to offer, and is still going strong — all of these cultures have something to offer specifically to the rune user, as if any culture wasn't worth investigating.

In the modern age, it is hard to truly grasp how the ancient mind worked, as we now live quite separated from our environment. Dry warm houses and comfortable cars shield us from the elements that birthed us. Dipping our feet into the writings of our collective past is a huge step towards engaging with what makes us what we truly are.


## What Next - Literally reading the Runes


I wanted to mention the actual reading of archaeological finds. It is a challenge, but rewarding.

Elder Futhark texts are very rare; much more common are texts written in Either the Younger Futhark or the Anglo-Saxon Futhark.

Annoyingly, there are even mixed stones with different sets mingled and sometimes possibly naively implemented. Words are frequently not separated, or kept to one line, and bind-runes are commonly used in writing to save on carving time.

There are more problems. Many of these stones are damaged, and writing on stone is no mean feat in the first place. Hopefully you begin to see the challenge. Also, the spelling ability of Vikings was erratic, many words never becoming standardised universally in runic.

It is likely that you will not understand the messages unless you know a bit of Old Norse, Icelandic, or possibly a mixture of other Germanic languages such as Norwegian, Swedish, or Danish and Anglo Saxon.

So it's hard.

But after saying all of this, some of us find it fun, myself included. These languages are closely related enough to English (particularly Northern and Scots dialects) for some words at least to leap out at you .'dottir' for daughter, 'bruthur' for brother, 'stain' or 'stein' for stone and 'eftir' for after, and the like. Just pronouncing them is fun too, and seeing how much you can get right.

Younger Futhark runes feature frequently on standing stones found all over northern Europe, but most commonly in Sweden, Norway, or Denmark. There are also some stunning Anglo Saxon Rune relics in Britain - Franks Casket, and the Ruthwell Cross shouting out as great examples.

Seeing and reading these ancient words also begins the road to Etymology, the study of the origins of words, which isn't given justice by the words 'fascinating' or 'insightful'. Fun fact: the word 'Asa' has parallels with the Hittite word 'Hassa' for god, and the Etruscan 'Aesir', also for god, suggesting a common origin.

I am at the 'pretty good at guessing' stage with ancient carvings, as I am fairly terrible at learning new languages.

I can only offer a first faltering step, but the Viking younger Futhark is worth sharing here, and a sample message in that script. Please take into account that there are university courses in this subject, so this page really is a very basic introduction, if that.

The example that I have chosen is an inscription carved on the romantically named 'u91', a memorial rune stone which can be found in Funbo in Uppland, Sweden. It is a nice easy one, and it's pretty.

You'll note that the writing rolls around the stone changing orientation as it goes, and is damaged in parts.

I initially read it thus:

*Thiafa auk funar raisti stain aftir uathr bruthur sin*

It's formal transcription is thus:

*Thiak auk kunar raisti stana aftir uathr bruthur sin*

This tanslates into English thus:

*Thiak and Kunar raised stone after Uathr their brother*

I got lucky here and recognised the word 'aftir', or sometimes 'eftir', and 'stana' or 'stain' along with 'bruthur'.

These words made it into the English language as 'after', 'stone' and 'brother'. I also got lucky with the word 'auk', in that the Eddia features this word fairly often. This word simply means 'and'.

You'll note that I stumbled because the rune Kaon was inverted and not wildly different from Feoh here - I wanted to keep my errors to give you that stumbling feeling.

The word 'sin' also baffled me at the time, particularly as the Sig rune is not particularly well formed. I was unfamiliar with that word, so I had to look it up. It appears to mean 'their'.

The name 'Thiak' or 'Thiafa' is on a damaged area of the stone. Annoyingly, there appears to be other heavily damaged runes before the 'th' as well as after the 'k', but the first rune, if anything, looks like Peorth and the last one possibly Ansur. As stated earlier, Elder Futhark runes do appear on younger Futhark scripts from time to time.

I described this as easy didn't I? It is definitely one of the easier ones.

I am afraid that I was unable to find an ancient Elder Futhark example that I was legally able to share, sure enough to read, and trusting enough of the formal translation.

I should mention that it is fun, if sometimes a bit cringe-worthy, to read modern runic jewellery, - lots of this is written in the Elder Futhark. Some of these have some fairly comedic spelling too (as would mine, should I ever get the chance).

## *What next - Explore*

Finally, using the Runes is also a great introduction to other magical systems. An adept rune user is not starting from scratch with Tarot or any other form of magic. Changing your mind set to match that of the peoples who developed each system is an important skill you will have learned — as is the ability to marry their beliefs with your own subjective world experience.

As already stated, be careful when drawing analogies between systems, as different systems are not always entirely compatible - yet seeing these mismatches is in itself an illuminating experience. Knowing that the sun is seen as man in Greece and woman in Japan gives you insight into different thought structures.

Of note, learning other systems will also benefit your rune skills. My favourite question of, 'What is missing?' comes to mind. If tarot or I-Ching can say something, how do the Runes say it, or do they have a different perspective? Why? Their incompatibilities are every bit the godsend that their perfect fits would have been.

I have personally found that as I grew to know the Runes, a lot of my personal use became internal. The Runes are kind of embedded in my mind as thought processes and logical tools, so my need to carry out runic rituals isn't what it once was — I do most of them in my head. I also pray to the gods, which you are welcome to take either as a proud declaration or a humble confession.

If you connect with either the Runes or the gods, a lot of your experimentation will have to be independent. Indeed, a lot of people will think you are a loony.

First of all, get used to that, and try to use it to make you a little more tolerant of other "loonies". Like you, they may have a point or two worth absorbing.

Most importantly, don't treat your belief system like some god-awful football team. The Runes are not anti-science, they are their own science. Neither do you or they need blind faith; keep questioning and keep your mind open to new ideas. You will serve your own ideals better if you are not an obviously impenetrable wall of ignorance, and if you truly wish to undermine a value, it is usually much more fragile from its own viewpoint.

Know this — it can be good being a 'fool', so enjoy it. Stepping off the trodden path is a risky, but great way to see things in a different light; learning to think on your own and measure concepts independently, learning to discern what you're thinking from what you're just repeating can only be a good thing.

I also ironically think that this true step away from the norm should encourage a tolerance to other cultures. Personally, I find as much alien in conventional western society as I do in Islam, Juju or Hinduism, and enjoy learning about all of these examples. Again, they give me another angle from which to study any problem.

# Bibliography

Not all of these resources have been directly referenced in my work, but they are part of my continuing formal education in the ways of the Runes.

## *Mythological material*

These books all relate to my education in the mythologies of the Europeans, although some of them may seem connected rather obscurely.

- *Edda* by Snorri Sturluson translated by Anthony Faulkes, published by The Everyman     Library in 1987
- *The Poetic Edda* translated by Carolyne Larrington published by The Oxford     University Press in 1999
- *The Poetic Edda: Stories of the Norse Gods and Heroes* by Jackson Crawford, Hackett Publishing Co, Inc (2015)
- *A is for Ox: A Short History of the Alphabet* by Lyn Davies, Folio Society (2006)
- *Myths of the Norsemen* by H.A. Guerber, published by Harrap &CO (undated)
- *Asgard and the Norse Heroes* retold by K.F.Boult, published by Everyman's Library     (undated)
- *Myths and Legends* by A. Horowitz, published by Story Library in 1991
- *Understanding your cat* by M.W.Fox, published by Blond & Briggs in 1974
- *Germania* by Tacitus
- *Gallica* by Julius Ceasar
- *Anglo-Saxon Poetry* by R.K.Gordon, published by Everyman in 1926
- *Fairies and Enchanters* by Amabel Williams-Ellis, published by Thomas Nelson & Sons

# Rune material

The following books refer more closely to my knowledge of the Runes.

- *Northern mysteries and magick* by Freya Aswynn, published by Llewelwyn
- *The complete illustrated guide to RUNES* by Nigel Pennick, published by Element in 1999
- *Practical magic in the Northern Tradition* by Nigel Pennick, published by Aquarian
- *Time keeping, and Star-Craft in the Northern Tradition* by Nigel Pennick, published by Aquarian
- *The secret lore of the Runes and other alphabets* by Nigel Pennick, published by Llewelwyn
- *The book of Runes* by Ralph Blum, first published by Oracle Books in 1982
- *The Complete guide to the Runes* by Tony Willis, published by Aquarian
- *Casting the Runes* by David and Julia Line published by Aquarian

# Internet Sources

The World Wide Web has also been used but selectively, as I do not completely trust much of it.

I detail one or two of my more trusted sources.

- https://sacred-texts.com/ - a great site with many translations of ancient texts available to the general public.
- http://omniglot.com - listing alphabets, and a brief history of their uses and origins
- http://northvegr.org - good pagan people (as far as I know) with useful source materials on-site.

- https://youtube.com/c/JacksonCrawford - Real expertise in Norse language and myth, free of both ivory tower elitism and the agendas of self-appointed gurus.
- http://aswynn.co.uk - Freya Aswyn is a renowned Odinic priestess with a great   knowledge of Rune-lore.
- https://etymonline.com/ -a site exploring the origins of words, and a great resource.

# Appendices

What appendices are these? I am lucky enough to be able to include the Norwegian and Icelandic rune poems. While they both deal with the Younger Futhark, and are thought to be considerably younger than the *Anglo-Saxon Rune Poem*, they are 'must haves' for a book on runes in my opinion. Also, because these are quite small, I am able to provide them in their original languages too, which is just fascinating. Note all that rhyming that I mentioned earlier.

Both of these poems were translated by Bruce Dickins at the turn of the 20th century. The originals are written in the Latin alphabet, and Roman and Christian imagery abounds.

I've also added some sections of W. H. Auden's translations from the *Elder Edda;* the collection of poems which play such a huge role in what we now have to understand this ancient culture.

The imagery present in the Runes is given a little colour, in that the expectations and portent of these ideas are explained a little by these poems.

Again, I advise getting a full modern copy of the *Elder Edda.* W H Auden's translation is not particularly respected in modern academic circles, as liberties were taken by the author.

We have already discussed the idea of 'kennings'. When a poem was considered artfully written, you frequently got two meanings where one would normally be. Often these 'kennings' were imposed by the very strict structure of the poem. In order to follow these strict rules of rhyme and metre, the author was forced to use associations - which in their own right store a deal of the author's psyche, if nothing else. By re-allocating or ignoring the strict metre of the poems, a lot of this material is rendered invisible and confusing by Auden's translation. He also had a habit of softening a lot of the grittier stuff.

However, remembering when I was learning this stuff makes me want to provide this older translation as a head start. It is also fun.

# The Norwegian Rune Poem

This, and the Icelandic Rune poem that follows, accompany the Younger Futhark - both at least appear to be younger than the Anglo-Saxon Rune poem, with written copies dating somewhere between the thirteenth and sixteenth century.

However, you'll note similarities in meaning, which hints at the original authors being aware of other texts or sharing an older source.

Note the Christian imagery herein.

| | | |
|---|---|---|
| Wealth is a source of discord among kinsmen; the wolf lives in the forest. | ᚠ | Fé vældr frænda róge; føðesk ulfr í skóge. |
| Dross comes from bad iron; the reindeer often races over the frozen snow. | ᚢ | Úr er af illu jarne; opt løypr ræinn á hjarne. |
| Giant causes anguish to women; misfortune makes few men cheerful. | ᚦ | Þurs vældr kvinna kvillu; kátr værðr fár af illu. |
| Estuary is the way of most journeys; but a scabbard is of swords. | ᚨ | Óss er flæstra færða fo,r; en skalpr er sværða. |
| Riding is said to be the worst thing for horses; Reginn forged the finest sword. | ᚱ | Ræið kveða rossom væsta; Reginn sló sværðet bæzta. |
| Ulcer is fatal to children; death makes a corpse pale. | ᚲ | Kaun er barna bo,lvan; bo,l gørver nán fo,lvan. |
| Hail is the coldest of grain; Christ created the world of old. | ᚼ | Hagall er kaldastr korna; Kristr skóp hæimenn forna. |
| Constraint gives scant choice; a naked man is chilled by the frost. | ᚾ | Nauðr gerer næppa koste; nøktan kælr í froste. |

| English | Rune | Old Norse |
|---|---|---|
| Ice we call the broad bridge; the blind man must be led. | ᛁ | Ís ko,llum brú bræiða; blindan þarf at læiða. |
| Plenty is a boon to men; I say that Frothi was generous. | ᚨ | Ár er gumna góðe; get ek at o,rr var Fróðe. |
| Sun is the light of the world; I bow to the divine decree. | ᛋ | Sól er landa ljóme; lúti ek helgum dóme. |
| Tyr is a one-handed god; often has the smith to blow. | ᛏ | Týr er æinendr ása; opt værðr smiðr blása. |
| Birch has the greenest leaves of any shrub; Loki was fortunate in his deceit. | ᛒ | Bjarkan er laufgrønstr líma; Loki bar flærða tíma. |
| Man is an augmentation of the dust; great is the claw of the hawk. | ᛦ | Maðr er moldar auki; mikil er græip á hauki. |
| A waterfall is a River which falls from a mountain-side; but ornaments are of gold. | ᛚ | Lo,gr er, fællr ór fjalle foss; en gull ero nosser. |
| Yew is the greenest of trees in winter; it is wont to crackle when it burns. | ᛣ | Ýr er vetrgrønstr viða; vænt er, er brennr, at svið |

# The Icelandic Rune Poem

You'll note here that the last line of each verse is not translated. These obscure lines seem to be a mixture of Roman and Icelandic in both imagery and language, making translation hard. Possibly, this is purposeful. Or possibly the writer is trying to connect with Roman magic.

I've had a go at trying to translate these myself and seemed to do ok, but I am not a scholar of Latin or Icelandic, so I consider it better for me not to tamper with the original.

| Wealth is source of discord among kinsmen and fire of the sea and path of the serpent. | ᚠ | Fé er frænda róg ok flæðar viti ok grafseiðs gata aurum fylkir. |
| Shower is lamentation of the clouds and ruin of the hay-harvest and abomination of the shepherd. | ᚢ | Úr er skýja grátr ok skára þverrir ok hirðis hatr. umbre vísi |
| Giant is torturer of women and cliff-dweller and husband of a giantess. | ᚦ | Þurs er kvenna kvöl ok kletta búi ok varðrúnar verr. Saturnus þengill. |
| God is aged Gautr and prince of Ásgarðr and lord of Vallhalla. | ᚨ | Óss er algingautr ok ásgarðs jöfurr, ok valhallar vísi. Jupiter oddviti. |
| Riding is joy of the horsemen and speedy journey and toil of the steed. | ᚱ | Reið er sitjandi sæla ok snúðig ferð ok jórs erfiði. iter ræsir. |
| Ulcer is disease fatal to children and painful spot and abode of mortification. | ᚲ | Kaun er barna böl ok bardaga [för] ok holdfúa hús. flagella konungr. |

Hail is cold grain
and shower of sleet
and sickness of serpents.

ᚼ

Hagall er kaldakorn
ok krapadrífa
ok snáka sótt.
grando hildingr.

Constraint is grief of the bond-maid
and state of oppression
and toilsome work.

ᚾ

Nauð er Þýjar þrá
ok þungr kostr
ok vássamlig verk.
opera niflungr.

Ice is bark of rivers
and roof of the wave
and destruction of the doomed.

ᛁ

Íss er árbörkr
ok unnar þak
ok feigra manna fár.
glacies jöfurr.

Plenty is boon to men
and good summer
and thriving crops.

ᛅ

Ár er gumna góði
ok gott sumar
algróinn akr.
annus allvaldr.

Sun is shield of the clouds
and shining ray
and destroyer of ice.

ᛋ

Sól er skýja skjöldr
ok skínandi röðull
ok ísa aldrtregi.
rota siklingr.

Týr is god with one hand
and leavings of the wolf
and prince of temples.

ᛏ

Týr er einhendr áss
ok ulfs leifar
ok hofa hilmir.
Mars tiggi.

Birch is leafy twig
and little tree
and fresh young shrub.

ᛒ

Bjarkan er laufgat lim
ok lítit tré
ok ungsamligr viðr.
abies buðlungr.

Man is delight of man
and augmentation of the earth
and adorner of ships.

ᛘ

Maðr er manns gaman
ok moldar auki
ok skipa skreytir.
homo mildingr.

Water is eddying stream
and broad geysir
and land of the fish.

ᛚ

Lögr er vellanda vatn
ok viðr ketill
ok glömmungr grund.
lacus lofðungr.

Yew is bent bow
and brittle iron
and giant of the arrow.

ᛦ

Ýr er bendr bogi
ok brotgjarnt járn
ok fífu fárbauti.
arcus ynglingr.

271

# The Anglo-Saxon Rune Poem

Finally, there is the *Anglo-Saxon Rune Poem* that plays such a large role in this book. The dark horse of this collection, it is dated to roughly 900 CE or older by many scholars, which would make it much older than the other rune poems, and possibly even the *Eddas*. As already mentioned the original was destroyed, and what we have is thought to be a transcription of a transcription. The 1706 transcription, has the rune names scrawled around the runes themselves, and not in the verse, but these are usually added to the verse in modern prints. I have compromised here with a colon to separate them.

While copying this through I was very conscious of the fact that this ancestor of the English language was harder for me to follow and indeed validate than the Norse equivalents. Also the original doesn't glaringly follow any rhyme or metre to my eyes. This posed a challenge when trying to present it here. However, I still could not resist the urge to get as close to the source as I can. This poem is in every other sense the easiest to follow, as well as the most informative. Hopefully the raw Anglo-Saxon will help keener minds than mine.

| | | |
|---|---|---|
| Wealth is a comfort to all men; yet must every man bestow it freely, if he wish to gain honour in the sight of the Lord. | ᚠ | Feoh: byþ frofur fira gehwylcum; sceal ðeah manna gehwylc miclun hyt dælan gif he wile for drihtne domes hleotan. |
| The aurochs is proud and has great horns; it is a very savage beast and fights with its horns; a great ranger of the moors, it is a creature of mettle. | ᚢ | Ur: byþ anmod ond oferhyrned, felafrecne deor, feohteþ mid hornum mære morstapa; þæt is modig wuht. |
| The thorn is exceedingly sharp, an evil thing for any knight to touch, uncommonly severe on all who sit among them. | ᚦ | Ðorn: byþ ðearle scearp; ðegna gehwylcum anfeng ys yfyl, ungemetum reþe manna gehwylcum, ðe him mid resteð. |
| The mouth is the source of all language, a pillar of wisdom and a comfort to wise men, a blessing and a joy to every knight. | ᚩ | Os: byþ ordfruma ælere spræce, wisdomes wraþu ond witena frofur and eorla gehwam eadnys ond tohiht. |

Riding seems easy to every
warrior while he is indoors
and very courageous to him
who traverses the high-roads
on the back of a stout horse.
The torch is known to every
living man by its pale, bright flame;
it always burns where princes sit within.

ᚱ Rad: byþ on recyde rinca gehwylcum
sefte ond swiþhwæt, ðamðe sitteþ on
ufan
meare mægenheardum ofer milpaþas.

ᚲ Cen: byþ cwicera gehwam, cuþ on fyre
blac ond beorhtlic, byrneþ oftust
ðær hi æþelingas inne restaþ.

Generosity brings credit and
honour, which support one's dignity;
it furnishes help and subsistence
to all broken men who are
devoid of aught else.
Bliss he enjoys who knows
not suffering, sorrow nor anxiety,
and has prosperity and
happiness and a good enough house.

ᚷ Gyfu: gumena byþ gleng and herenys,
wraþu and wyrþscype and wræcna
gehwam
ar and ætwist, ðe byþ oþra leas.

ᚹ Wenne: bruceþ, ðe can weana lyt
sares and sorge
and him sylfa hæfþ blæd and blysse and
eac byrga geniht.

Hail is the whitest of grain;
it is whirled from the vault of heaven
and is tossed about by gusts of wind
and then it melts into water.

ᚺ Hægl: byþ hwitust corna;
hwyrft hit of heofones lyfte,
wealcaþ hit windes scura;
weorþeþ hit to wætere syððan.

Trouble is oppressive to the heart;
yet often it proves a source of
help and salvation
to the children of men, to
everyone who heeds it betimes.
Ice is very cold and immeasurably slippery;
it glistens as clear as glass and
most like to gems;
it is a floor wrought by the frost,
fair to look upon.
Summer is a joy to men, when
God, the holy King of Heaven,
suffers the earth to bring forth shining fruits
for rich and poor alike.

ᚾ Nyd: byþ nearu on breostan; weorþeþ
hi þeah oft niþa bearnum
to helpe and to hæle gehwæþre, gif hi
his hlystaþ æror.

ᛁ Is: byþ ofereald, ungemetum slidor,
glisnaþ glæshluttur gimmum gelicust,
flor forste geworuht, fæger ansyne.

ᛄ Ger: byÞ gumena hiht, ðonne God
læteþ,
halig heofones cyning, hrusan syllan
beorhte bleda beornum ond ðearfum.

The yew is a tree with rough bark,
hard and fast in the earth,
supported by its roots,
a guardian of flame and a joy upon an estate.

ᛇ Eoh: byþ utan unsmeþe treow,
heard hrusan fæst, hyrde fyres,
wyrtrumun underwreþyd, wyn on eþle.

Peorth is a source of recreation
and amusement to the great,
where warriors sit blithely
together in the banqueting-hall.

ᛈ Peorð: byþ symble plega and hlehter
wlancum [on middum], ðar wigan
sittaþ
on beorsele bliþe ætsomne.

The Eolh-sedge is mostly to be
found in a marsh;
it grows in the water and makes a ghastly wound,
covering with blood every warrior
who touches it.

ᛉ

Eolh:-secg eard hæfþ oftust on fenne
wexeð on wature, wundaþ grimme,
blode breneð beorna gehwylcne
ðe him ænigne onfeng gedeþ.

The sun is ever a joy in the hopes of
seafarers
when they journey away over the fishes' bath,
until the courser of the deep bears them to
land.

ᛋ

Sigel: semannum symble biþ on hihte,
ðonne hi hine feriaþ ofer fisces beþ,
oþ hi brimhengest bringeþ to lande.

Tiw is a guiding star;
well does it keep faith with princes;
it is ever on its course over the
mists of night and never fails.

ᛏ

Tir: biþ tacna sum,
healdeð trywa wel wiþ æþelingas;
a biþ on færylde ofer nihta genipu,
næfre swiceþ.

The poplar bears no fruit; yet
without seed it brings forth suckers,
for it is generated from its leaves.
Splendid are its branches and gloriously adorned
its lofty crown which reaches to the skies.

ᛒ

Beorc: byþ bleda leas, bereþ efne swa
ðeah
tanas butan tudder, biþ on telgum wlitig,
heah on helme hrysted fægere,
geloden leafum, lyfte getenge.

The horse is a joy to princes in the presence of
warriors.
A steed in the pride of its hoofs,
when rich men on horseback bandy words about it;
and it is ever a source of comfort to the restless.

ᛗ

Eh: byþ for eorlum æþelinga wyn,
hors hofum wlanc, ðær him hæleþ
ymb[e]
welege on wicgum wrixlaþ spræce
and biþ unstyllum æfre frofur.

The joyous man is dear to his kinsmen;
yet every man is doomed to fail his fellow,
since the Lord by his decree will
commit the vile carrion to the earth.

ᛗ

Man: byþ on myrgþe his magan leof:
sceal þeah anra gehwylc oðrum swican,
forðum drihten wyle dome sine
þæt earme flæsc eorþan betæcan.

The ocean seems interminable to men,
if they venture on the rolling bark
and the waves of the sea terrify them
and the courser of the deep heed not its bridle.

ᛚ

Lagu: byþ leodum langsum geþuht,
gif hi sculun neþan on nacan tealtum
and hi sæyþa swyþe bregaþ
and se brimhengest bridles ne gym[eð].

Ing was first seen by men among
the East-Danes,
till, followed by his chariot,
he departed eastwards over the waves.
So the Heardingas named the hero.

ᛝ

Ing: wæs ærest mid East-Denum
gesewen secgun, oþ he siððan est
ofer wæg gewat; wæn æfter ran;
ðus Heardingas ðone hæle nemdun.

An estate is very dear to every man,
if he can enjoy there in his house
whatever is right and proper in
constant prosperity.

ᛟ

Eþel: byþ oferleof æghwylcum men,
gif he mot ðær rihtes and gerysena on
brucan on bolde bleadum oftast.

Day, the glorious light of the
Creator, is sent by the Lord;
it is beloved of men, a source of
hope and happiness to rich and
poor, and of service to all.

ᛞ

Dæg: byþ drihtnes sond, deore
mannum,
mære metodes leoht, myrgþ and tohiht
eadgum and earmum, eallum brice.

The oak fattens the flesh of pigs
for the children of men.
Often it traverses the gannet's bath,
and the ocean proves whether
the oak keeps faith in honourable fashion.
The ash is exceedingly high
and precious to men.
With its sturdy trunk it offers
a stubborn resistance,
though attacked by many a man.
Yr is a source of joy and
honour to every prince and knight;
it looks well on a horse and is
a reliable equipment for a journey.

Iar is a river fish and yet it
always feeds on land;
it has a fair abode
encompassed by water, where
it lives in happiness.
The grave is horrible to every knight,
when the corpse quickly begins to cool
and is laid in the bosom of the dark earth.
Prosperity declines, happiness
passes away and covenants are broken.

ᚪ Ac: byþ on eorþan elda bearnum
flæsces fodor, fereþ gelome
ofer ganotes bæþ; garsecg fandaþ
hwæþer ac hæbbe æþele treowe.

ᚫ Æsc: biþ oferheah, eldum dyre
stiþ on staþule, stede rihte hylt,
ðeah him feohtan on firas monige.

ᛣ Yr: byþ æþelinga and eorla gehwæs
wyn and wyrþmynd,
byþ on wicge fæger,
fæstlic on færelde, fyrdgeatewa sum.

ᛡ Iar: byþ eafix and ðeah a bruceþ
fodres on foldan, hafaþ fægerne eard
wætre beworpen, ðær he wynnum
leofaþ.

ᛠ Ear: byþ egle eorla gehwylcun,
ðonn[e] fæstlice flæsc onginneþ,
hraw colian, hrusan ceosan
blac to gebeddan; bleda gedreosaþ,
wynna gewitaþ, wera geswicaþ.

# *The Havamal (Translated by W.H.Auden)*

Young and alone on a long road,
Once I lost my way:
Rich I felt when I found another;
Man rejoices in man,
A kind word need not cost much,
The price of praise can be cheap:
With half a loaf and an empty cup
I found myself a friend,
Two wooden stakes stood on the plain,
On them I hung my clothes:
Draped in linen, they looked well born,
But, naked, I was a nobody
Too early to many homes I came,
Too late, it seemed, to some:
The ale was finished or else un-brewed,
The unpopular cannot please,
Some would invite me to visit their homes,
But none thought I needed a meal,
As though I had eaten a whole joint,
Just before with a friend who had two
The man who stands at a strange threshold,
Should be cautious before he cross it,
Glance this way and that:
Who knows beforehand what foes may sit
Awaiting him in the hall?
Greetings to the host,
The guest has arrived,
In which seat shall he sit?
Rash is he who at unknown doors
Relies on his good luck,
Fire is needed by the newcomer
Whose knees are frozen numb;

Meat and clean linen a man needs
Who has fared across the fells,
Water, too, that he may wash before eating,
Handcloth's and a hearty welcome,
Courteous words, then courteous silence
That he may tell his tale,
Who travels widely needs his wits about him,
The stupid should stay at home:
The ignorant man is often laughed at
When he sits at meat with the sage,
Of his knowledge a man should never boast,
Rather be sparing of speech
When to his house a wiser comes:
Seldom do those who are silent Make mistakes;
mother wit Is ever a faithful friend,
A guest should be courteous
When he comes to the table
And sit in wary silence,
His ears attentive,
his eyes alert:
So he protects himself,
Fortunate is he who is favoured in his lifetime
With praise and words of wisdom:
Evil counsel is often given
By those of evil heart,
Blessed is he who in his own lifetime
Is awarded praise and wit,
For ill counsel is often given
By mortal men to each other,
Better gear than good sense
A traveller cannot carry,
Better than riches for a wretched man,
Far from his own home,
Better gear than good sense
A traveller cannot carry,
A more tedious burden than too much drink

A traveller cannot carry,
Less good than belief would have it
Is mead for the sons of men:
A man knows less the more he drinks,
Becomes a befuddled fool,
I-forget is the name men give the heron
Who hovers over the fast:
Fettered I was in his feathers that night,
When a guest in Gunnlod's court
Drunk I got, dead drunk,
When Fjalar the wise was with me:
Best is the ban quet one looks back on after,
And remembers all that happened,
Silence becomes the Son of a prince,
To be silent but brave in battle:
It befits a man to be merry and glad
Until the day of his death,
The coward believes he will live forever
If he holds back in the battle,
But in old age he shall have no peace
Though spears have spared his limbs
When he meets friends, the fool gapes,
Is shy and sheepish at first,
Then he sips his mead and immediately
All know what an oaf he is,
He who has seen and suffered much,
And knows the ways of the world,
Who has travelled, can tell what spirit
Governs the men he meets,
Drink your mead, but in moderation,
Talk sense or be silent:
No man is called discourteous who goes
To bed at an early hour
A gluttonous man who guzzles away
Brings sorrow on himself:
At the table of the wise he is taunted often,

Mocked for his bloated belly,
The herd knows its homing time,
And leaves the grazing ground:
But the glutton never knows how much
His belly is able to hold,
An ill tempered, unhappy man
Ridicules all he hears,
Makes fun of others, refusing always
To see the faults in himself
Foolish is he who frets at night,
And lies awake to worry,
A weary man when morning comes,
He finds all as bad as before,
The fool thinks that those who laugh
At him are all his friends,
Unaware when he sits with wiser men
How ill they speak of him.
The fool thinks that those who laugh
At him are all his friends:
When he comes to the Thing and calls for support,
Few spokesmen he finds
The fool who fancies he is full of wisdom
While he sits by his hearth at home.
Quickly finds when questioned by others.
That he knows nothing at all.
The ignorant booby had best be silent
When he moves among other men,
No one will know what a nit-wit he is
Until he begins to talk;
No one knows less what a nit-wit he is
Than the man who talks too much.
To ask well, to answer rightly,
Are the marks of a wise man:
Men must speak of men's deeds,
What happens may not be hidden.
Wise is he not who is never silent,

Mouthing meaningless words:
A glib tongue that goes on chattering
Sings to its own harm.
A man among friends should not mock another:
Many believe the man
Who is not questioned to know much
And so he escapes their scorn.
An early meal a man should take
Before he visits friends,
Lest, when he gets there,
he go hungry,
Afraid to ask for food.
The fastest friends may fall out
When they sit at the banquet-board:
It is, and shall be, a shameful thing
When guest quarrels with guest,
The wise guest has his way of dealing
With those who taunt him at table:
He smiles through the meal,
not seeming to hear
The twaddle talked by his foes.
The tactful guest will take his leave Early,
not linger long:
He starts to stink who outstays his welcome
In a hall that is not his own.
A small hut of one's own is better,
A man is his master at home:
A couple of goats and a corded roof
Still are better than begging.
A small hut of one's own is better,
A man is his master at home:
His heart bleeds in the beggar who must
Ask at each meal for meat.
A wayfarer should not walk unarmed,
But have his weapons to hand:
He knows not when he may need a spear,

Or what menace meet on the road.
No man is so generous he will jib at accepting
A gift in return for a gift,
No man so rich that it really gives him
Pain to be repaid.
Once he has won wealth enough,
A man should not crave for more:
What he saves for friends, foes may take;
Hopes are often liars.
With presents friends should please each other,
With a shield or a costly coat:
Mutual giving makes for friendship,
So long as life goes well,
A man should be loyal through life to friends,
To them and to friends of theirs,
But never shall a man make offer
Of friendship to his foes.
A man should be loyal through life to friends,
And return gift for gift,
Laugh when they laugh,
but with lies repay
A false foe who lies.
If you find a friend you fully trust
And wish for his good-will,
exchange thoughts,
exchange gifts,
Go often to his house.
If you deal with another you don't trust
But wish for his good-will,
Be fair in speech but false in thought
And give him lie for lie.
Even with one you ill-trust
And doubt what he means to do,
False words with fair smiles
May get you the gift you desire.
To a false friend the footpath winds

Though his house be on the highway.
To a sure friend there is a short cut,
Though he live a long way off.
Hotter than fire among false hearts burns
Friendship for five days,
But suddenly slackens when the sixth dawns:
Feeble their friendship then.
The generous and bold have the best lives,
Are seldom beset by cares,
But the base man sees bogies everywhere
And the miser pines for presents.
The young fir that falls and rots
Having neither needles nor bark,
So is the fate of the friendless man:
Why should he live long?
Little a sand-grain, little a dew drop,
Little the minds of men:
All men are not equal in wisdom,
The half-wise are everywhere
It is best for man to be middle-wise,
Not over cunning and clever:
The fairest life is led by those
Who are deft at all they do.
It is best for man to be middle-wise,
Not over cunning and clever:
No man is able to know his future,
So let him sleep in peace.
It is best for man to be middle-wise,
Not over cunning and clever:
The learned man whose lore is deep
Is seldom happy at heart.
Brand kindles brand till they burn out,
Flame is quickened by flame:
One man from another is known by his speech
The simpleton by his silence.
Early shall he rise who has designs

On another's land or life:
His prey escapes the prone wolf,
The sleeper is seldom victorious.
Early shall he rise who rules few servants,
And set to work at once:
Much is lost by the late sleeper,
Wealth is won by the swift,
A man should know how many logs
And strips of bark from the birch
To stock in autumn, that he may have enough
Wood for his winter fires.
Washed and fed,
one may fare to the Thing:
Though one's clothes be the worse for Wear,
None need be ashamed of his shoes or hose,
Nor of the horse he owns,
Although no thoroughbred.
As the eagle who comes to the ocean shore,
Sniffs and hangs her head,
Dumfounded is he who finds at the Thing
No supporters to plead his case.
It is safe to tell a secret to one,
Risky to tell it to two,
To tell it to three is thoughtless folly,
Everyone else will know.
Often words uttered to another
Have reaped an ill harvest:
Two beat one, the tongue is head's bane,
Pockets of fur hide fists.
Moderate at council should a man be,
Not brutal and over bearing:
Among the bold the bully will find
Others as bold as he.
These things are thought the best:
Fire, the sight of the sun,
Good health with the gift to keep it,

And a life that avoids vice.
Not all sick men are utterly wretched:
Some are blessed with sons,
Some with friends,
some with riches,
Some with worthy works.
The halt can manage a horse,
the handless a flock,
The deaf be a doughty fighter,
To be blind is better than to burn on a pyre:
There is nothing the dead can do.
It is always better to be alive,
The living can keep a cow.
Fire, I saw, warming a wealthy man,
With a cold corpse at his door.
A son is a blessing, though born late
To a father no longer alive:
Stones would seldom stand by the highway
If sons did not set them there.
He welcomes the night who has enough provisions
Short are the sails of a ship,
Dangerous the dark in autumn,
The wind may veer within five days,
And many times in a month.
The half-wit does not know that gold
Makes apes of many men:
One is rich, one is poor
There is no blame in that.
Cattle die, kindred die,
Every man is mortal:
But the good name never dies
Of one who has done well
Cattle die, kindred die,
Every man is mortal:
But I know one thing that never dies,
The glory of the great dead

Fields and flocks had Fitjung's sons,
Who now carry begging bowls:
Wealth may vanish in the wink of an eye,
Gold is the falsest of friends.
In the fool who acquires cattle and lands,
Or wins a woman's love,
His wisdom wanes with his waxing pride,
He sinks from sense to conceit.
Now is answered what you ask of the runes,
Graven by the gods,
Made by the All Father,
Sent by the powerful sage:
It. is best for man to remain silent.
For these things give thanks at nightfall:
The day gone, a guttered torch,
A sword tested, the troth of a maid,
Ice crossed, ale drunk.
Hew wood in wind-time,
in fine weather sail,
Tell in the night time tales to house-girls,
For too many eyes are open by day:
From a ship expect speed, from a shield, cover,
Keenness from a sword,
but a kiss from a girl.
Drink ale by the hearth, over ice glide,
Buy a stained sword, buy a starving mare
To fatten at home: and fatten the watch-dog.
Trust not an acre early sown,
Nor praise a son too soon:
Weather rules the acre, wit the son,
Both are exposed to peril,
A snapping bow, a burning flame,
A grinning wolf, a grunting boar,
A raucous crow, a rootless tree,
A breaking wave, a boiling kettle,
A flying arrow, an ebbing tide,

A coiled adder, the ice of a night,
A bride's bed talk, a broad sword,
A bear's play, a prince's children,
A witch's welcome, the wit of a slave,
A sick calf, a corpse still fresh,
A brother's killer encountered upon
The highway a house half-burned,
A racing stallion who has wrenched a leg,
Are never safe: let no man trust them.
No man should trust a maiden's words,
Nor what a woman speaks:
Spun on a wheel were women's hearts,
In their breasts was implanted caprice,
To love a woman whose ways are false
Is like sledding over slippery ice
With unshod horses out of control,
Badly trained two-year-olds,
Or drifting rudderless on a rough sea,
Or catching a reindeer with a crippled hand
On a thawing hillside: think not to do it.
Naked I may speak now for I know both:
Men are treacherous too
Fairest we speak when falsest we think:
many a maid is deceived.
Gallantly shall he speak and gifts bring
Who wishes for woman's love:
praise the features of the fair girl,
Who courts well will conquer.
Never reproach another for his love:
It happens often enough
That beauty ensnares with desire the wise
While the foolish remain unmoved.
Never reproach the plight of another,
For it happens to many men:
Strong desire may stupefy heroes,
Dull the wits of the wise

The mind alone knows what is near the heart,
Each is his own judge:
The worst sickness for a wise man
Is to crave what he cannot enjoy.
So I learned when I sat in the reeds,
Hoping to have my desire:
Lovely was the flesh of that fair girl,
But nothing I hoped for happened.
I saw on a bed Billing's daughter,
Sun white, asleep:
No greater delight I longed for then
Than to lie in her lovely arms.
Come Odin, after nightfall
If you wish for a meeting with me:
All would be lost if anyone saw us
And learned that we were lovers.
Afire with longing I left her then,
Deceived by her soft words:
I thought my wooing had won the maid,
That I would have my way.
After nightfall I hurried back,
But the warriors were all awake,
Lights were burning, blazing torches:
So false proved the path
Towards daybreak back I came
The guards were sound asleep:
I found then that the fair woman
Had tied a bitch to her bed.
Many a girl when one gets to know her
Proves to be fickle and false:
That treacherous maiden taught me a lesson,
The crafty woman covered me with shame
That was all I got from her.
Let a man with his guests be glad and merry,
Modest a man should be
But talk well if he intends to be wise

And expects praise from men:
Fimbul fambi is the fool called
Unable to open his mouth.
Fruitless my errand, had I been silent
When I came to Suttung's courts:
With spirited words I spoke to my profit
In the hall of the aged giant.
Rati had gnawed a narrow passage,
Chewed a channel through stone,
A path around the roads of giants:
I was like to lose my head
Gunnlod sat me in the golden seat,
Poured me precious mead:
Ill reward she had from me for that,
For her proud and passionate heart,
Her brooding foreboding spirit.
What I won from her I have well used:
I have waxed in wisdom since I came back,
bringing to Asgard Odrerir,
the sacred draught.
Hardly would I have come home alive
From the garth of the grim troll,
Had Gunnlod not helped me, the good woman,
Who wrapped her arms around me.
The following day the Frost Giants came,
Walked into Har's hall To ask for Har's advice:
Had Bolverk they asked, come back to his friends,
Or had he been slain by Suttung?
Odin, they said, swore an oath on his ring:
Who from now on will trust him?
By fraud at the feast he befuddled Suttung
And brought grief to Gunnlod.
It is time to sing in the seat of the wise,
Of what at Urd's Well I saw in silence,
saw and thought on.
Long I listened to men

Runes heard spoken, (counsels revealed.)
At Har's hall, In Har's hall:
There I heard this.
Loddfafnir, listen to my counsel:
You will fare well if you follow it,
It will help you much if you heed it.
Never rise at night unless you need to spy
Or to ease yourself in the outhouse.
Shun a woman, wise in magic,
Her bed and her embraces:
If she cast a spell, you will care no longer
To meet and speak with men,
Desire no food, desire no pleasure,
In sorrow fall asleep.
Never seduce anothers wife,
Never make her your mistress.
If you must journey to mountains and firths,
Take food and fodder with you.
Never open your heart to an evil man
When fortune does not favour you:
From an evil man, if you make him your friend,
You will get evil for good.
I saw a warrior wounded fatally
By the words of an evil woman
Her cunning tongue caused his death,
Though what she alleged was a lie.
If you know a friend you can fully trust,
Go often to his house
Grass and brambles grow quickly
Upon the untrodden track.
With a good man it is good to talk,
Make him your fast friend:
But waste no words on a witless oaf,
Nor sit with a senseless ape.
Cherish those near you, never be
The first to break with a friend:

Care eats him who can no longer
Open his heart to another.
An evil man, if you make him your friend,
Will give you evil for good:
A good man, if you make him your friend
Will praise you in every place,
Affection is mutual when men can open
All their heart to each other:
He whose words are always fair
Is untrue and not to be trusted.
Bandy no speech with a bad man:
Often the better is beaten
In a word fight by the worse.
Be not a cobbler nor a carver of shafts,
Except it be for yourself:
If a shoe fit ill or a shaft be crooked
The maker gets curses and kicks.
If aware that another is wicked, say so:
Make no truce or treaty with foes.
Never share in the shamefully gotten,
But allow yourself what is lawful.
Never lift your eyes and look up in battle,
Lest the heroes enchant you,
who can change warriors
Suddenly into hogs,
With a good woman, if you wish to enjoy
Her words and her good will,
Pledge her fairly and be faithful to it:
Enjoy the good you are given,
Be not over wary, but wary enough,
First, of the foaming ale,
Second, of a woman wed to another,
Third, of the tricks of thieves.
Mock not the traveller met On the road,
Nor maliciously laugh at the guest:
Scoff not at guests nor to the gate chase them,

But relieve the lonely and wretched,
The sitters in the hall seldom know
The kin of the new-comer:
The best man is marred by faults,
The worst is not without worth.
Never laugh at the old when they offer counsel,
Often their words are wise:
From shrivelled skin, from scraggy things
That hand among the hides
And move amid the guts,
Clear words often come.
Heavy the beam above the door;
Hang a horse-shoe On it
Against ill-luck, lest it should suddenly
Crash and crush your guests.
Medicines exist against many evils:
Earth against drunkenness, heather against worms
Oak against costiveness, corn against sorcery,
Spurred rye against rupture, runes against bales
The moon against feuds, fire against sickness,
Earth makes harmless the floods.
Wounded I hung on a wind-swept gallows
For nine long nights,
Pierced by a spear, pledged to Odin,
Offered, myself to myself
The wisest know not from whence spring
The roots of that ancient rood
They gave me no bread,
They gave me no mead,
I looked down;
with a loud cry
I took up runes;
from that tree I fell.
Nine lays of power
I learned from the famous Bolthor, Bestla's father:
He poured me a draught of precious mead,

Mixed with magic Odrerir.
Waxed and throve well;
Word from word gave words to me,
Deed from deed gave deeds to me,
Runes you will find, and readable staves,
Very strong staves,
Very stout staves,
Staves that Bolthor stained,
Made by mighty powers,
Graven by the prophetic god,
For the gods by Odin, for the elves by Dain,
By Dvalin, too, for the dwarves,
By Asvid for the hateful giants,
And some I carved myself:
Thund, before man was made, scratched them,
Who rose first, fell thereafter
Know how to cut them, know how to read them,
Know how to stain them, know how to prove them,
Know how to evoke them, know how to score them,
Know how to send them, know how to send them,
Better not to ask than to over-pledge
As a gift that demands a gift,
Better not to send than to slay too many,
The first charm I know is unknown to rulers
Or any of human kind;
Help it is named,
for help it can give In hours of sorrow and anguish.
I know a second that the sons of men
Must learn who wish to be leeches.
I know a third: in the thick of battle,
If my need be great enough,
It will blunt the edges of enemy swords,
Their weapons will make no wounds.
I know a fourth:
it will free me quickly
If foes should bind me fast

With strong chains, a chant that makes Fetters spring from the feet,
Bonds burst from the hands.
I know a fifth: no flying arrow,
Aimed to bring harm to men,
Flies too fast for my fingers to catch it
And hold it in mid-air.
I know a sixth:
it will save me if a man
Cut runes on a sapling's Roots
With intent to harm; it turns the spell;
The hater is harmed, not me.
If I see the hall
Ablaze around my bench mates,
Though hot the flames, they shall feel nothing,
If I choose to chant the spell.
I know an eighth:
that all are glad of,
Most useful to men:
If hate fester in the heart of a warrior,
It will soon calm and cure him.
I know a ninth:
when need I have
To shelter my ship on the flood,
The wind it calms, the waves it smoothes
And puts the sea to sleep,
I know a tenth:
if troublesome ghosts
Ride the rafters aloft,
I can work it so they wander astray,
Unable to find their forms,
Unable to find their homes.
I know an eleventh:
when I lead to battle Old comrades in-arms,
I have only to chant it behind my shield,
And unwounded they go to war,
Unwounded they come from war,

U unscathed wherever they are.
I know a twelfth:
If a tree bear
A man hanged in a halter,
I can carve and stain strong runes
That will cause the corpse to speak,
Reply to whatever I ask.
I know a thirteenth
if I throw a cup Of water over a warrior,
He shall not fall in the fiercest battle,
Nor sink beneath the sword,
I know a fourteenth, that few know:
If I tell a troop of warriors
About the high ones, elves and gods,
I can name them one by one.
(Few can the nit-wit name.)
I know a fifteenth,
that first Thjodrerir
Sang before Delling's doors,
Giving power to gods, prowess to elves,
Fore-sight to Hroptatyr Odin,
I know a sixteenth:
if I see a girl
With whom it would please me to play,
I can turn her thoughts, can touch the heart
Of any white armed woman.
I know a seventeenth:
if I sing it,
the young Girl will be slow to forsake me.
I know an eighteenth that I never tell
To maiden or wife of man,
A secret I hide from all
Except the love who lies in my arms,
Or else my own sister.
To learn to sing them, Loddfafnir,
Will take you a long time,

Though helpful they are if you understand them,
Useful if you use them,
Needful if you need them.
The Wise One has spoken words in the hall,
Needful for men to know,
Unneedful for trolls to know:
Hail to the speaker,
Hail to the knower,
Joy to him who has understood,
Delight to those who have listened.

# The Song of the Sybil or Voluspa (Translated by W H Auden & P B Taylor)

Heidi men call me when their homes I visit,
A far seeing Volva, wise in talismans.
Caster of spells, cunning in magic,
To wicked women welcome always.
Arm rings and necklaces, Odin you gave me,
To learn my lore, to learn my magic:
Wider and wider through all worlds I see.
Outside I sat by myself when you came,
Terror of the gods, and gazed in my eyes.
What do you ask of me? Why tempt me?
Odin, I know where your eye is concealed,
Hidden away in the well of Mimir:
Mimir each morning his mead drinks
From Valfather's pledge. Well would you know more?
Of Heimdal too and his horn I know.
Hidden under the holy tree
Down on it pours a precious stream from Valfather's pledge
Well would you know more?
Silence I ask of the sacred folk,
Silence of the kith and kin of Heimdal:
At your will Valfather, I shall well relate
The old songs of men I remember best.
I tell of giants from times forgotten.
Those who fed me in former days:
Nine worlds I can reckon, nine roots of the tree.
The wonderful ash, way under the ground
When Ymir lived long ago,
Was no sand or sea, no surging waves.
Nowhere was there earth nor heaven above.
Bur a grinning gap and grass nowhere.
The sons of Bur then built up the lands.

Moulded in magnificence middle-Earth:
Sun stared from the south on the stones of their hall,
From the ground there sprouted green leeks.
Sun turned from the south, sister of Moon,
Her right arm rested on the rim of Heaven;
She had no inkling where her hall was,
Nor Moon a notion of what might he had,
The planets knew not where their places were.
The high gods gathered in council,
In their hall of judgement. all the rulers:
To Night and to Nightfall their names gave,
The Morning they named and the Mid-Day,
Mid-Winter, Mid-Summer, for the assigning of years.
At Ida's Field the Aesir met:
Temple and altar they timbered and raised,
Set up a forge to smithy treasures,
Tongs they fashioned and tools wrought;
Played chess in the court and cheerful were;
Gold they lacked not, the gleaming metal
Then came three, the Thurs maidens,
Rejoicing in their strength, from Giant-home.
The high Gods gathered in council.
In their hall of judgement: Who of the dwarves
Should mould man by master craft
From Brimir's blood and Blain' s limbs?
Motsognir was their mighty ruler,
Greatest of dwarves, and Durin after him:
The dwarves did as Durin directed,
Many man forms made from the earth.
Nyi and Nidi, Nordri, Sudri, Austri and Vestri, Althjof, Dvalin,
Bivor,
Bavor Bombur, Nori, An and Anar, Ai, Mjodvitnir, Veignr and
Gandalf,
Vindalf, Thorin, Thror and Thrain, Thekkur, Litur, Vitur, Nar
and Nyradur,

Fili, Kili, Fundin, Nali Hefti, Vili, Hanar, Sviur, Billing, Bruni, Bildur,
and Buri, Frar, Hornbori Fraegur, Loni, Aurvangur, Jari, Eikinskjaldi:
(All Durin's folk I have duly named,)
I must tell of the dwarves in Dvalin' s host;
Like lions they were in Lofar's time:
In Juravale's marsh they made their dwelling,
From their Stone hall set out on journeys,
There was Draupnir and Dolgthrasir, Har, Haugspori,
Hlevangur, Gloi, Dori,
Ori, Dufur, Andvari, Skirvir, Virvir Skafidur, Ai, Alf and Yngvi,
Eikinskjaldi, Fjalar and Frosti, Finn and Ginnar: Men will remember while
men live
The long line of Lofar's forbears.
Then from the host three came,
Great, merciful, from the God's home:
Ash and Elm on earth they found,
Faint, feeble, with no fate assigned them
Breath they had not, nor blood nor senses,
Nor language possessed, nor life-hue:
Odin gave them breath, Haenir senses,
Blood and life hue Lothur gave.
I know an ash tree, named Yggdrasil:
Sparkling showers are shed on its leaves
That drip dew, into the dales below,
By Urd's well it waves evergreen,
Stands over that still pool,
Near it a bower whence now there come
The Fate Maidens, first Urd,
Skuld second, scorer of runes,
Then Verdandi, third of the Norns:
The laws that determine the lives of men
They fixed forever and their fate sealed.
The first war in the world I well remember,

When Gullveig was spitted on spear-points
And burned in the hall of the high god:
Thrice burned, thrice reborn,
Often laid low, she lives yet,
The gods hastened to their hall of judgement,
Sat in council to discover who
Had tainted all the air with corruption
And Odhinn's maid offered to the giants,
At the host Odin hurled his spear
In the first world-battle; broken was the plankwall
Of the gods fortress: the fierce Vanes
Caused war to occur in the fields.
The gods hastened to their hall of judgement,
Sat in council to discover who
Had tainted all the air with corruption
And Odhinn's maid offered to the giants.
One Thorr felled in his fierce rage;
Seldom he sits when of such he hears:
Oaths were broken, binding vows,
Solemn agreements sworn between them.
Valkyries I saw, coming from afar,
Eagerly riding to aid the Goths;
Skuld bore one shield, Skogul another
Gunn, Hild, Gondul and Spearskogul:
Duly have I named the daughters of Odin,
The valiant riders the Valkyries.
Baldur I saw the bleeding God,
His fate still hidden, Odhinn's Son:
Tall on the plain a plant grew,
A slender marvel, the mistletoe.
From that fair shrub, shot by Hodur,
Flew the fatal dart that felled the god,
But Baldur' s brother was born soon after:
Though one night old, Odhinn's Son
Took a vow to avenge that death.
His hands he washed not nor his hair combed.

Till Baldur's bane was borne to the pyre:,
Deadly the bow drawn by Vali,
The strong string of stretched gut,
But Frigga wept in Fensalir
For the woe of Valhalla. Well, would you know more?
I see one in bonds by the boiling springs;
Like Loki he looks, loathsome to view:
There Sigyn sits, sad by her husband,
In woe by her man. Well would you know more?
From the east through Venom Valley runs
Over jagged rocks the River Gruesome.
North, in Darkdale, stands the dwelling place
Of Sindri's kin, covered with gold;
A hall also in Everfrost,
The banquet hall of Brimir the giant.
A third I see, that no sunlight reaches,
On Dead Man's Shore: the doors face northward,
Through its smoke vent venom drips,
Serpent skins enskein that hall.
Men wade there tormented by the stream,
Vile murderers, men forsworn
And artful seducers of other mens wives:
Nidhogg sucks blood from the bodies of the dead
The wolf rends them. Well, would you know more?
In the east dwells a crone, in Ironwood:
The brood of Fenris are bred there
Wolf-monsters, one of whom
Eventually shall devour the sun.
The giants watchman, joyful Eggthur
Sits on his howe and harps well:
The red cock, called All-Knower
Boldly crows from Birdwood.
Goldencomb to the gods crows
Who wakes the warriors in Valhalla:
A soot red hen also calls
From Hel's hall, deep under the ground.

Loud howls Garm before Gnipahellir,
Bursting his fetters, Fenris runs:
Further in the future afar I behold
The twilight of the gods who gave victory.
Brother shall strike brother and both fall,
Sisters' sons defiled with incest;
Evil be on earth, an age of. Whoredom,
Of sharp sword-play and shields clashing,
A wind-age, a wolf-age till the world ruins:
No man to another shall mercy show.
The waters are troubled, the waves surge up:
Announcing now the knell of Fate,
Heimdal winds his horn aloft,
On Hel's road all men tremble
Yggdrasil trembles, the towering ash
Groans in woe; the wolf is loose:
Odin speaks with the head of Mimir
Before he is swallowed by Surt's kin.
From the east drives Hrym, lifts up his shield
The squamous serpent squirms with rage
The great worm with the waves contending
The pale-beaked eagle pecks at the dead,
Shouting for joy: the ship Naglfar
Sails out from the east, at its helm Loki
With the children of darkness, the doom-bringers
Offspring of monsters, allies of the wolf,
All who Byleists's brother follow.
What of the gods? What of the elves?
Gianthome groans the gods are in council
The dwarves grieve before their door of stone,
Masters of walls. Well, would you know more?
Surt with the bane of branches comes
From the south, on his sword the sun of the Valgods,
Crags topple, the crone falls headlong,
Men tread Hel's road, the Heavens split open.
A further woe falls upon Hlin

As Odin comes forth to fight the wolf;
The killer of Beli battles with Surt:
Now shall fall Frigga's beloved.
Now valiant comes Valfather's son,
Vidar, to vie with Valdyr in battle,
Plunges his sword into he son of Hvedrung,
Avenging his father with a fell thrust.
Now the son of Hlodyn and Odin comes
To fight with Fenris; fiercest of warriors
He mauls in his rage all Middle-Earth;
Men in fear all flee their homesteads;
Nine paces back steps Bur's son
Retreats from the worm of taunts unafraid.
Now death is the portion of doomed men,
Red with blood the buildings of gods,
The sun turns black in the summer after,
Winds whine. Well, would know more?
Earth sinks in the sea, the sun turns black,
Cast down from Heaven are the hot stars,
Fumes reek, into flames burst,
The sky itself is scorched with fire.
I see Earth rising a second time
Out of the foam, fair and green;
Down from the fells fish to capture,
Wings the eagle; waters flow.
At lda's Field the Aesir meet:
They remember the worm of Middle-Earth,
Ponder again the great twilight
And the ancient runes of the high god
Boards shall be found of a beauty to wonder at,
Boards of gold in the grass long after,
The chess boards they owned in the olden days,
Unsown acres shall harvests bear,
Evil be abolished, Baldur return
And Hropt's hall with Hod rebuild,
Wise gods. Well, would you know more?

Haenir shall wield the wand of prophecy,
The sons two brothers set up their dwelling
In wide Windhome. Well, would you know more?
Fairer than sunlight, I see a hall
A hall thatched with gold in Gimle:
Kind Lords shall live there in delight for ever.
Now rides the Strong One to Rainbow Door,
Powerful from heaven, the All-Ruler:
From the depths below a drake comes flying
The dark dragon from Darkfell,
Bears on his opinions the bodies of men,
Soars overhead I sink now.

# SIGDRIFUMAL *(Translated by W. H. Auden & P. B. Taylor)*

Sigurd rode up to Hindfell and headed south towards
Frankland.
On the mountain he saw a bright light like a fire burning and
shining towards Asgardhr. But when he arrived he found a
shield-wall and over it a banner. Sigurd went to the shield-wall
and saw a man in full armour lying asleep. He took the helmet
from his head whereupon he saw that it was a woman.
The byrnie was stuck fast as if it had grown into her flesh.
With his sword Grani he slit the byrnie through from the neck
down and through both sleeves, and removed it from her.
She awoke, sat up and said:

Who has slit my byrnie and from sleep roused me?
Who has broken the spell that bound me so long?

Sigmund's son, Sigurd, who lately,
Killed the Raven's Carrion Tree.

Long have I slept, long was I sleeping,
Long are the miseries of men: Odin chose to charm me to
sleep,
When he spoke a spell over me.

Sigurd sat down and asked her her name.
She took a horn full of mead and gave him a remembrance
drink.

Hail Day, Hail, Sons of Day!
Hail Night and New Moon!
With kind eyes look hither and grant us
Victory while we live.

Hail Gods! Hail Goddesses!
Hail bountiful Earth!
Grace us both with the gift of speech,
And leech hands while we live.


Her name was Sigrdrifa, meaning Victory-Granter, and she was
a Valkyrie.
She said that two kings had fought.
One was named Helm Gunnar; he had grown old but was still
the greatest warriors, and to him Odin had decreed victory.
The other Agnar, Hauda's brother, who never had hopes of
being favoured.
Victory-Granter felled Helm Gunnar in battle.
In revenge Odin pricked her with a sleep thorn and said that
she should never there-after fight for victory but should be
married. But, she said him, I in my turn bind myself by a vow
to marry no man except one who knows no fear.
Sigurd asked her to make her wisdom known to him, since she
had knowledge of all the worlds, Sigrdrifa said:


Sea runes you should know to save from wreck
Sail steeds on the Sea:
Carve them on the bow and the blade of the rudder,
Etch them with fire on the oars;
Though high the breakers and blue the waves.
You shall sail safe into harbour.


Limb-runes you should know if a leech you would be,
Who can properly probe wounds:
It is best to carve them on the bark of trees,
Whose limbs lean to the east.


Speech-runes you should know, so that no man
Out of hatred may do you harm:
These you shall wind, these you shall fold,
These you shall gather together,
When the people throng to the Thing to hear

Just judgements given.

Thought-runes you should know if you would be thought by all
The wisest of mortal men:
Hropt devised them,
Hropt scratched them,
Hropt took them to heart.
From the wise waters the waters then run,
From the head of Heidraupnir,
From the horn of Hoddrofnir.

On the Ben he stood with Brimir's sword,
A helmet upon his head:
Then Mimir's head uttered for the first time
Words of great wisdom.

He spoke runes on the shied that stands before the shining god,
In the ear of Early Awake and on the hoof of All-Wise
On the wheel that turns ever under Hrungnir's chariot,
On the sled straps and on Sleipnir's teeth.

On the bears paw and on Bragi's tongue,
On the wolfs foot and the falcons beak,
On the bloody wings and at the bridges end,
On the palm of child loosener and the path of comfort.

On glass and on gold and the fore-guesses of men,
In wine and in malt and in the mind's seat,
On Gungnir's point and on Grani's breast,
On the nails of the Norns and the Night Owls beak.

All were scratched off which were scratched on,
Mingled with holy mead
And sent on the wide ways,
Some to gods some to elves,

Some to the wise Vanes,
Some to the sons of men.

There are Beech runes, there are Birth Runes,
And all the ale runes
Precious runes of power!
Unspoiled they are unspoiled they are,
Learn them and use them long
Till the high powers perish.

Now you shall choose, for the choice is given you,
Maple - of - well - forged - weapons,
Speech or silence, you shall say which:
Evil is allotted to all.

I shall not flee, though fated to die,
For never have I known fear.
Grant me but this give me all
Your love counsel while I live.

I counsel you first, among kinsmen remain
Free from fault and reproach:
Be slow to wrath though they wrong you much,
This will do you good in death.

I counsel you second; swear no oath
But what you mean to abide by:
A halter awaits the word breaker,
Villainous is the wolf-of-vows.

I counsel you third; at the Thing never bandy
Words with unwise men,
For the unwise man often speaks
worse words than he knows.

But speak your mind; of the silent it is often
Believed they are low-born cowards,

That their foes are speaking the truth.
Famous-at-home may fail abroad
When strangers test his truth:
The reward of the liar is not long in coming;
He dies the very next day.

I say to you fourth; if a sorceress dwell,
A witch by the way side,
It is better to leave than to be her guest
Though night fall on your faring.

Fore sighted eyes need the sons of men
Whenever they come to combat;
By the broad road may sit bale wise women
Who blunt both blades and courage.

I counsel you fifth; though fair be the maids
On the benches within the hall,
Let your sleep not be ruled by the silver of marriage,
Nor beguile the girls with kisses.

I counsel you sixth; if you sit with warriors
And the ale talk turns ill,
Bandy no words with bragging drunkards:
Wine steals the wits of many.

Quarrels and ale have often been
The cause of ill to heroes:
Death to some, to some bewitchment,
Many are the grief's of men.

I counsel you seventh; if you Come disputing
With fierce hearted fighters,
To battle is better than to be burned in the hall,
Although it gleam with gold.

I counsel you eighth; of evil beware,

Of charming smiles of deceit:
Let no maidens entice you, nor men's wives,
Nor lead them into lawless pleasures.

I counsel you ninth; cover the dead
Whenever on earth you find them,
Be they dead of sickness. or drowned in the river,
Or warriors slain by weapons.

Dead corpses you should clean with water,
Wash their hands and heads,
Comb and dry them. in their coffins lay them,
And bid them a blessed sleep.

I counsel you tenth; trust not ever
the words of a wolf's kin,
If you have killed his kin
Or felled his father:
Wolf's bane is in his blood
Though he be glad of your gold.

Anger and hate are ever awake,
So is harm also:
The boar visored, when vain-glorious.
Lack both wit and weapons.

I counsel you eleventh; there lurks evil
Round each bend of the road:
A long life you must not look to have,
So great are the hatreds grown.

# Acknowledgements

I'd like to thank a few people. Peter Burnett, my publisher either made or saved this book by showing an interest in something initially presented as bones to pick for another potential project. His belief and support here has had a value that frankly I will struggle to measure. He also shared the mixed pleasure of proofing and editing this beast, a challenge only for the brave.

And then there was the full time editing and typesetting team.

Ambrose Kelly, thank you for going through my book so carefully and humouring my hoards of stupid questions. There are about a page's worth of commas in this book that owe their good home to Ambrose, and about a chapter more that had to go. Know her pain.

Joshua Andrew, Thank you for the layout and type-setting as well as additional proofing. This heavily illustrated book went through many renditions and last minute edits, often initiating another reshuffle. Additions, subtractions, rephrasing; If you can think of a way for an author to be a pain in the neck, I've probably done it.

Thanks to Martin Page for much needed pep talk and sound advice.

Lastly I need to thank my wife, Louise, and son, Rowyn. They have endured a lot throughout the writing this book. My reading the whole thing aloud thousands of times, a studio in the living room, intense jubilation, intense despair, lots of scribbling, and my personality. I have reliably been a challenge to live with, and my time as an author has been no less challenging. Also thanks to: Mum and Dad, My elder sons Jamie and Daniel, Ailsa Frew, Shihab Ahmed, Daniel Hemingway, Penny Hodson, David Wilson, The Leith Collective, All at The Edinburgh Literary Salon, and the Heretics A little hello to Jethro, who has been not helped writing this book at all, but is an almost bottomless source of learning and inspiration.